HAVE A GOOD MOURNING

HAVE A GOOD MOURNING

17 SURPRISING WAYS LOSS CAN LEAD TO INSPIRATION, HOPE AND JOY

JENNIFER E. HALE

NEW DEGREE PRESS

HAVE A GOOD MOURNING

17 Surprising Ways Loss Can Lead to Inspiration, Hope and Joy

ISBN   978-1-64137-514-6   *Paperback*

978-1-64137-515-3   *Kindle Ebook*

978-1-64137-516-0   *Ebook*

For my mother, Suzanne "Sue" M. Hale, whose love, memory, and spirit could fill a million books. Thank you for bringing so much joy and meaning into my life then, now, and forever.

With Love Forever, Your Jenny

CONTENTS

——

ACKNOWLEDGMENTS

"It takes a village to raise a child."

—AFRICAN PROVERB

While I don't have children of my own yet, this book is the closest I've come to such a blessing. Truth be told, I could never have raised it without the tremendous village of remarkable people who supported, loved, and guided me along this journey. I proudly acknowledge each and every person listed here for their commitment to helping me bring this book to life.

First and foremost, I would like to thank God for blessing me with a wonderful, amazing mother, whose boundless love provided me with inspiration to write this book, and for the constant love, healing, and strength He gives me every day.

Next, I would like to thank my incredible family for supporting and encouraging me, especially my wonderful, amazing, loving father, Jeff Hale, who unconditionally and generously supported me from Day 1. I would also like to thank my amazing sisters, Amanda Taylor and Becky Hale, for their love, support, and guidance along the way. I would like to thank my sweet nephew and niece, Nik and Liddy Taylor, for filling my heart with the utmost joy during this process, too. A very warm and heartfelt thanks to all of my loving, supportive family including Mary and Bob Murray, Scott Murray, Pat Hale, Karen Hale, Tony Hale, Sandra Glatz, Ryan Glatz, and Mary Garvey.

I would like to extend a very special thanks to my wonderful boyfriend, Marc Stichion, who supported me through every stage of my book-writing journey with grace, patience, and love. I would also like to thank his loving family Rhonda Stichion, Terry Schunck, and Diane Schunck for their support.

I'd like to give a special shout-out to my dear friend, Tanya Alvarez, the founder of OwnersUp. From the moment I met her, this fearless, incredible woman pushed me out of my comfort zone in tremendous ways and challenged me to do things I never thought were possible, including writing this book. She even put me in touch with several of the amazing people whose stories are featured in this book.

I wish to acknowledge all of my incredible friends from Notre Dame of Maryland University, including Tabatha Brooks, Jacquelin "Jackie" Morrison, Tiffany Clough-Busko, Susan Davis, Aliza Ross, Irene McNulty, and Maria Iannuccillo, SSND.

I would like to personally recognize my lovely friends from Alter Communications, Inc., including Rebecca Addington, Jessica Toutsis, Claudia Meyers, and Cortney Geare.

A very hearty and special thanks to all of my incredibly generous and wonderful Agora friends, including Laura Cadden, Danielle O'Dell, William "Bill" Patalon III, Kerri Shannon, Kelly Higginbotham, Julie Hassett, Carolynn Ananian, Bill Spencer, Rebecca Kerins, Molly Ward, Bret Holmes, Joanne Zucker, Laura Amos, and Melissa Schoepflin.

I would like to thank my very generous and amazing SAIC friends, including Sarah Fooks, Cara Cole, and Erin Mettee for their support as well as all of my incredible friends from Landmark Worldwide, including Jen Coken, Amanda Bullock, Dannielle VonDerLinden, DPM, Deanna Pharis, Jonathan Kittrell, Yolanda McLaughlin, Raymond Nelson, Rajika Mahan, Ashley Fetty, Natasha Peeples, Michael Nelson, and Carol Schubert.

A special thanks to my childhood friends and very special friends from the Norrisville community, including Barbara Neville, Lindsay Neville, Jamie Hollandsworth, Maggie Mundle, Megan Bredlow, and Megan Louderback.

I would like to extend a warm thank you to my Team and Training comrades, Darin Messer and Bobby Marsee, and my Laughter Yoga friends, Lameteria Hall and Josephene Smythe-Brown.

I want to thank each and every one of my mom's nursing friends and colleagues, including Christine Baldwin, Jackie

Kretsch, Vickie Bands, Donna Enright, Mary Kendall, Lori Conley, Nancy Howard, Phyllis Jones, and Barbara Wishart.

A special thanks to Tammi Nash, Jamie Nash, Wanda Goldschmidt, Liz Entin, Lindsay Roberts, Kathryn King, Jean Kimmel, Tanya Alvarez, Anna Taylor, Rob and Tina Carestia, Dan Benjamin, David and Chelsea Hintze, Donna Audia, Mary McQuaige, Barbara MacStravic Burgett, Jill Sanchez, Clint Eltringham, Karen Marsee-Branstetter, and Craig Morsberger for their generous support.

I would like to express my great appreciation to everyone at New Degree Press for their encouragement, support, and enthusiasm during my book-writing journey, including Eric Koester, Brian Bies, Stephen Howard and Stephanie McKibben. I would like to offer my special thanks to my co-authors and dear friends, Natalie Sanchez and Jennifer Garman, for supporting me and for enriching my experience with the program.

I would also like to thank the people I interviewed, including Jennifer Morilla, Sarah Fooks, Jen Coken, Kinja Dixon, Michael Tesalona, Nathasha Alvarez, Carrie Brady, Gigi Trencher, Stephen Howard, Justin Thongsavanh, Anthony Samadani, Anisha Weimer, Dan Benjamin, Bobby Marsee, Barrett Pitner, Amanda Taylor, Jeff Hale, Natalie Sanchez, and Bill Spencer.

I would like to thank the wonderfully talented, patient miracle worker, Mary Ann Tate from The Art of Words, for reading, editing, and helping me craft every single word in this book. I will be forever grateful to her for her willingness to sacrifice her time and personal life to help me finish this book in a timely fashion. I would also like to thank William "Bill" Patalon III for believing in me and helping me write, edit, and shape the introduction as well as the first two chapters.

I would also like to recognize everyone else who is not mentioned here for all of their contributions to help me make this book a reality. I also appreciate everyone who helped spread the word about this book on social media.

THE MOURNING DOVE AWAKENING

"Owning our story can be hard but not nearly as difficult as spending our lives running from it."

—BRENÉ BROWN

I just remember I was thirsty.

So thirsty. And exhausted. The kind of exhausted where you have to *will* yourself to move. I padded to the kitchen of my parents' house, filled a small juice glass with tap water, and stole a glance at the infamous light-activated bird clock that has adorned the wall above the kitchen sink for twenty-five years.

I remember that it was 1:27 a.m. In three minutes, the Canada goose that lived in the clock would split the wee-morning quiet with its on-the-half-hour honk, so I twisted the knob on the dimmer just in the nick of time to give his honker a rest.

I turned and headed down the hall as I gulped a few unsatisfying mouthfuls of water. I really wanted to go straight to my bedroom that I'd slept in since I was five and collapse in the twin bed—a familiar, reassuring haven.

Something told me not to go to sleep yet. In a fatigued trance, I avoided my room and went to the one where my mom, Suzanne—or Sue as most people called her—was sleeping.

THE MOURNING DOVE

For three months, my mother had been battling something I had never even heard of before. Non-small cell adenocarcinoma. It's a rare lung cancer that targets women who are non-smokers. In my mother, it was now so advanced that the insidious attacker had invaded her liver, spine, and brain.

During a recent visit to Mom's oncologist, the defeated look in his eyes as he showed us the medical scans contradicted the encouraging words that accompanied his discussion of the treatment "game plan." I saw "hopeless" on his face, and I knew right then what the outcome would be. But my mom, dad, and sisters remained hopeful for a miracle.

The doctors gave her a chemo-and-radiation plan and sent her on her way. What they didn't give her was a "you have twelve months to live" timeframe. This wasn't an accidental omission. The reality was that Mom had almost no time left at all.

We took her home and pretended this was the proverbial "bad dream." We talked optimistically about the treatment plan and may have even promised to investigate clinical trials. It was just a front. The cancer wasn't just a Bad Dream. It was a nightmare, a full-blown horror movie. First, my mother lost her independence. Then her hair. And, ultimately, her capacity to hope.

And yet, there was one thing that this hideous raider didn't, and couldn't, take from Mom: her spunk.

Not long after this nightmare started, my dad, Jeff, had come home with a camper he'd bought on a whim. He parked it in the driveway, explaining it could serve as a guest house on wheels for Becky, my out-of-town baby sister. After he rambled through this explanation, Mom turned to me and muttered, "Your father is just like Huckleberry Finn. You never know what he's going to do next." At that exact moment, I realized I already missed my mom, and she wasn't even gone yet.

In addition to the spunk, there was a predictability to my mother, the good kind that might be better described as dependability. As friends, neighbors, her nursing co-workers, and customers of the family Christmas tree farm found out how sick she was, the get-well cards, help-you-out casseroles, gifts, flowers, and encouragement calls, texts, and emails rolled in like a flood tide.

True to form, Mom had one thing on her mind: thank-you notes, and lots of them. She wrote them herself for as long as she was able. And when she couldn't grip the pen anymore, she asked my older sister, Amanda, to take over. Mom tasked me, her middle daughter, with having lunch delivered to the infusion-center staff at Northern Maryland's Upper

Chesapeake Medical Center, as a tangible thank you for making her time there so comfortable.

Inevitably, there came a time when, to our heart-wrenching dismay, Mom stopped asking us for help. That's when she stopped doing anything. Soon after that, the cancer took over completely. And Mom fell into a coma. A deep one. At that point, Mom's hospice nurse, a kind, gentle woman named Karin, whom all of us had grown to love, prescribed morphine. The objective was to keep my mother comfortable and to help her "transition."

Transition.

That word is one of those loathsome bits of medical jargon that's intended to mask the tragic nature of what's actually happening. The more I heard that word, the more I hated it. It symbolized the end of my amazing mother's life. And it meant the end was near.

As I walked toward Mom's bed that morning, I was hoping it hadn't arrived. My sister Amanda, cousin Scott, and Aunt Mary were all in the room. Carefully, I crawled up into the bed and moved over next to her. She was still and almost lifeless. I wrapped my arms around her narrow, emaciated waist, held my head close to hers, and for the millionth time whispered, "I love you."

I watched her breathe. Once, twice, three times. Shallow. Very shallow. I waited for my mother's chest to rise again, waiting for her to take that next breath. She never did. Then it hit me. I'd watched my mother—the woman who'd raised me, cared for me, served as my sounding board and my inspiration for all of my thirty-one years—take her final breath. I watched my mother pass away. I watched her die.

It was like a switch had been flipped. For all those months that she'd fought her brutal battle with stage 4 lung cancer, I'd prayed for her to be freed from her agony. But from the moment she took that last breath, I ached. I instantly missed her. I ached for her loving touch, her warm hugs, her unsolicited advice, her early-morning texts—all the things that reached across the miles, the years, the changes.

My brain knew she was gone, but my heart couldn't let go. I had stayed with her until the end and I stayed with her even after the end. I stayed with her until my father and I watched as the two men from the funeral home wheeled her out the front door.

There was nothing I could do to bring her back. *Nothing.* Her life here with us was over.

I didn't know what to do with myself, so I walked back to her room and lay on her bed. Eventually, I drifted off to sleep as I hugged Snuggles, the big, fluffy, well-loved-and-not-so-white-or-soft-anymore teddy bear that had been mine since childhood. I had given him to Mom to hold when I couldn't be with her.

As remarkable as it sounds, I awoke to the birdsong of a mourning dove outside my mother's bedroom window. I often woke up to that cooing when I had come into Mom's bed for comfort from bad dreams as a child. That morning, the bird's gentle call was especially sweet. Its soft melody gave me hope and a message. It told me something important—that a new journey had begun.

A journey of reconciliation. A journey to make sense of it all. A journey of mourning.

A journey of *good* mourning.

That is what has brought me here—what brought me to you.

MY JOURNEY THROUGH GRIEF

My journey through the grieving process was one of self-discovery. The quest began that day. And it could have ended before it got very far. At first, I accepted a social worker's advice and tried to manage my grief the way she recommended. She was the expert, after all. I visited the prescribed counselors. I read the books. I even joined the support groups. But I soon realized something I couldn't ignore. It actually *alarmed* me. All these efforts actually made me feel… worse.

None of these remedies were having the expected results. The approach that was supposed to soothe my paralyzing pain and help me get on with my newly motherless life did not work for me. These techniques were all part of the grieving "process" the experts tell us to use. But they weren't helping. To be honest, I felt like I was going through the motions, and that made me feel worse. It raised uncomfortable questions.

Am I doing something wrong?

Is there something wrong with me?

Do I not fit the mold of a traditional grieving person?

I wanted more than these supposed one-size-fits-all grieving strategies might bring me. Something more than just a pat on the back and a tissue box.

At first, I ardently *welcomed* the sympathy I received.

I saw the shocked reactions of strangers in these support structures—the group sessions, one-on-one grief counseling, and private Facebook groups. They all seemed to only give me "permission" to wallow in my sorrow for yet another day. The stories from others who'd lost mothers or fathers super-charged a feeling I swore I'd never succumb to: a shameless act of self-pity. Their grief gave me a way to re-experience my own sadness and relive my debilitating heartache.

At the two-month mark after my mother's passing, I had become trapped in my grief. I finally had to pull the rip-cord. I had to coerce myself out of this wallowing-in-grief quagmire that had actually become quite the comfort zone for me. Unfortunately, I had no idea how to do so. I mean, I'd already read and done everything possible. *Hadn't I?* I scoured all the grief literature for addendums, references for clues on where to go next. I wanted to find a "Plan B" or a "Plan C" but found nothing.

Nothing.

Who could I turn to now? Who could be a "guide" to help me come to grips with, and accept, the loss of one of the two most important people in my life? Wasn't there anyone out there who could show me how to channel my pain and suffering into something positive, something constructive, something worthwhile—perhaps even something life-changing—so that I could experience the *good mourning* I was so desperately seeking?

I searched and came up empty.

I was dumbfounded. Could I really be the only person on earth experiencing this turmoil? I wanted to find a way to grieve—to mourn my mom's passing—in a way that didn't leave me feeling like I was being run over by a Mack truck (in forward and reverse) ten times an hour every hour since her death.

The fact is that nearly two people die every second.[1] And most of those people leave behind loved ones, each of whom is savaged by loss just as much as I was. That means that every second, innocent people, like you and me, are impacted by a loved one's death. And like an army of grieving lemmings, we all follow the same path of mourning and never really come to terms with the loved ones we lost. The belief that there's only one pathway to follow to mourn "properly" is just not true.

---

1   Medindia Content Team. "World Death Clock." Medindia.net, www. medindia.net/patients/calculators/world-death-clock.asp

Our counselors tell us about the five stages of grief: denial, anger, bargaining, depression, and acceptance. This is from the work done by Elisabeth Kübler-Ross, a Swiss-born psychiatrist and seminal thinker on dying and death. Before Kübler-Ross, people were expected to be stoic about death. It wasn't okay to talk about loss or grief, let alone display emotions such as sorrow. Her work opened up the discussions about death—and led to the support systems we have in place today.

Here's the kicker, and very few people are aware of this. In developing these stages, Kübler-Ross' goal was to describe the emotional process that terminally afflicted patients must navigate as they came to terms with their fatal malady. She wasn't trying to help us—the "mourners"—deal with the death of a loved one at all. She was helping those who were about to die. Over time, these five stages were applied to grieving, since the belief was that spouses, other family members, and friends seemed to experience similar emotions after losing a loved one. It was an easy transferal, according to a *Scientific American* report in 2008.[2]

Clinical psychologist David B. Feldman cautions the grieving process isn't quite so cleanly predictable. *"Studies now show that grievers don't progress through these stages in a lock-step fashion,"* Feldman wrote in a 2017 report in *Psychology*

---

2   Shermer, Michael. "Five Fallacies of Grief: Debunking Psychological Stages." Scientificamerican.com, www.scientificamerican.com/article/ five-fallacies-of-grief/

Today.[3] *"Consequently, when any of us loses someone we love, we may find that we fit the stages precisely as Kübler-Ross outlined, or we may skip all but one. We may race through them or drag our feet all the way to acceptance. We may even repeat or add stages that Kübler-Ross never dreamed of. In fact, the actual grief process looks a lot less like a neat set of stages and a lot more like a roller coaster of emotions. Even Kübler-Ross said that grief doesn't proceed in a linear and predictable fashion, writing toward the end of her career that she regretted her stages had been misunderstood."*

This "misunderstanding" has been damaging, even tragic. People already dealing with loss, perhaps even tragedy, are further burdened with the self-esteem-scuffing feeling of having "done it wrong." I had that experience as I watched my mother wither. And this confusion worsened after her passing. I cast about for a better approach. For a process or a compass or a roadmap that would help me find my way—but in the order I wanted and at the pace I wanted. I wanted to discover a way to mourn with joy.

The only way to truly find what I was looking for was to create it myself. In fact, you're holding it in your hands right now. What you have is my own invention, a way to actively take on mourning the loss of your loved one, as I did my mother's death. I call it: *Have a Good Mourning.* In this original design, I took the first letter of each of these words and made an acrostic. Each is a step to take to heal from your loss. I've

---

3   Feldman, David B. "Why the Five Stages of Grief Are Wrong." Psychologytoday.com, www.psychologytoday.com/us/blog/supersurvivors/201707/why-the-five-stages-grief-are-wrong

personally used each of these techniques to find joy again in my life.

The truth is, I have deliberately refused to track those "five stages of grief" after my mother died. I've refused to mourn in the "traditional" way. I've refused to obsess over her loss or to wallow in pain.

Here's a perfect example. Instead of classic black, I deliberately, even defiantly, picked out a cherry-red dress to wear to her wake and an emerald-green one paired with hot-pink pumps for her funeral. I definitely stood out—an oasis of splashy color against a black, dull backdrop. But the bright colors, I knew, symbolized my mother's warm smile. And I have yet to wear black since she died. The more color I wear, the better I feel. And I know Mom would approve.

THE ART OF *HAVING A GOOD MOURNING*

My *good mourning* practices, which I outline in this book, have brought me a lot of joy, but they've also made me realize one vital thing about grief. Each moment in your life—past, present, or future—pays homage to your loved one's legacy and how they helped shape you. If we cast a dark shadow over our lives with sadness, their light goes dim. When that happens, yours does, too.

I want you to have a different experience. I want you to remember, celebrate, and honor your loved one in a way that would not only make them proud but that will bring you joy and comfort. I want you to *"Have a Good Mourning,"* so I'm going to share this approach with you right now.

In the phrase *"Have a Good Mourning,"* I've paired each of the letters with a strategy that can be found in its own chapter. Each one will not only make you feel more connected to your loved one but will help you grow from your loss. But, most of all, you'll be able to do both with joy.

- **H**appiness: Find the one thing that gives you the most joy and hold onto it.
- **A**ction: Do something that helps others but also makes you feel great.
- **V**ictory: Celebrate big and small achievements every single day.
- **E**xpression: Speak your truth.
- **A**lliance: Find a supportive community that pushes you as you grow.
- **G**enerosity: Do something nice for others as often as you can.
- **O**penness: Open your eyes to possibilities that your loved one is nearby.
- **O**riginality: Find the thing that makes you "tick" and explore the possibilities.
- **D**etermination: Persevere no matter what.
- **M**emories: Keep your memories close to your heart as you bring them to life.
- **O**smosis: Share your loved one's gifts with the world.
- **U**niqueness: Forge a brand-new life path, if you so choose.
- **R**ituals: Allot time to celebrate your loved one.
- **N**ostalgia: Relive the fun times from your past.
- **I**nvention: Recreate a new you from the inside out.
- **N**urturing: Find healing in your caring for others.
- **G**reatness: Realize you're *much* stronger than you think.

If one of these piques your interest more than the others, just flip straight to the chapter and read away. I designed each story to stand on its own—and I did so with a purpose. I wanted to give you an array of *good mourning* practices to choose from because I've learned that one size doesn't actually fit all when it comes to mourning.

Each chapter introduces you to a fellow *good mourning-er* who, because they traveled their own path, has gotten the most out of their journey. Every person you'll meet gives an example of how to live out a *good mourning*. You'll see how Bobby Marsee, a dear friend of mine, used the power of "Alliance" to make a difference in his own life and thousands of others. I'll even send you on your way with a few *good mourning* insights at the end of each chapter to use as inspiration in your own life.

HOW TO READ THIS BOOK
"I'm nuts over you too, Jen."

That was the last email I received from my mother. After I told her I needed to lower my cholesterol, Mom sent me a health article about how nuts can help improve your HDL. That was Mom. As a loving mother and nurse, Mom couldn't help but help. When something went awry, she was there to commiserate, offer advice, give me hugs or, in the worst cases, help pick up the pieces.

In this case, instead of whipping me into a tizzy by stressing over my cholesterol, Mom simply showed me that eating a handful of almonds a day would help me better my health.

When I changed my mindset, and my actions, in response to my cholesterol, everything just fell into place.

The same is true for mourning. While we can't bring back the person we lost, we can change the way we look at, feel about, and react to the painful new void in our lives. And this loss, while uniquely painful, can still yield beautiful things: new friendships, new experiences, new challenges, and most of all, a new you. Once you envision all the goodness that can come after your loss, once you've experienced a *good mourning*, your life will change for the better.

Mine has.

After losing my mother, I set out on a mission to meet as many fellow people on the *good mourning* journey as possible. I not only wanted to meet them, but I also wanted to hear and record their incredible stories of triumph, success, and transformation.

You'll meet them, too.

In this book, you'll discover:

- How Kinja Dixon, a self-made millionaire and author of *Re-Creationism*, meaningfully reconnected with his late mother...
- How Jennifer Morilla, a Big Apple marketer, brings desperately needed clean water filters and a sense of caring to underdeveloped communities abroad...
- How Michael Tesalona, a web guru and *Ted Talk* speaker, feels his sister's presence wherever he goes...

In these pages, I also share my own *good mourning* journey with you. I explain how I became a proud sheep feeder, a camel enthusiast, a Laughter Yoga leader, a long-distance cyclist, and an author. But none of these things would have happened if I hadn't left room for myself to grow as I mourned. I had to escape the box of "conventional mourning" and get outside my own comfort zone to discover what was truly possible.

If you're searching for something different when it comes to mourning—an approach that permits you to remember your loved one while breaking free of paralyzing pain—you've come to the right place. If you want to mourn your loved one while remembering the things that brought you joy and to move on with acceptance and hope, *Have a Good Mourning* is for you.

I found that the concept of a *good mourning* has been around for a while. Part 1 explores the genesis of the *"good mourning"* process. Here you'll read about three fellow *good mourning-ers* from different points in history and learn how the practice of mourning has changed (or not!) through the centuries.

In part 2, we dive deep into the journey of mourning. You'll discover something incredibly powerful—something you may not even know you had—that will give you the strength to use your loss as a springboard into your new, transformed life. It's called the *"Good Mourning Shift."* It's deep inside all of us but is dormant until you access it. The chapters in this section will help you learn how to draw on this resource.

In part 3, you'll meet some pretty incredible people who, like you, have suffered a heartbreaking loss. But by following the *good mourning* practices explained in these chapters, you can develop the skills and the strength to leave your old grief-stricken life behind and embrace your new, joyful destiny as you heal, grow, and ultimately transform yourself for this bright future.

No matter where you are on your journey, there is always room to grow. I hope you are challenged by the insights that follow and are inspired to have a *good mourning*.

Let's get started…

PART 1

HISTORY OF THE *GOOD MOURNING* MOVEMENT

CHAPTER 1

THERE'S NO PLACE LIKE ROME

"While there's life, there's hope."

—MARCUS TULLIUS CICERO

I was a world-class fidgeter.

I squirmed on the hard, wooden pew inside St. Mary's Catholic Church, our parish nestled in a prolific cornfield just below the Mason-Dixon line. As I shuffled around, I saw that my mother was giving me the proverbial "hairy eyeball." I was on her *very* last nerve.

Mom whispered, out of the corner of her mouth, through clenched teeth, "Jennifer, you are on thin ice. If you pull on my arm one more time, your Nintendo privileges will be revoked… for a week."

No Mario? For an entire week?! That was unimaginable!

I tried my hardest to keep still and pay attention. But I couldn't wait for that 11:00 a.m. service to end. I knew we were "getting there." To the end, I mean. We just had to be. I remember that I took a quick peek at Mom's twenty-four-karat gold Timex wristwatch—the one she wore religiously after scoring it at a post-Christmas sale at the local Sears. It was... only 11:23? Oh, no! It *had* to be closer to noon than that. It was official. Time had stopped and my Nintendo privileges were doomed. There was no way I could survive for thirty-seven more minutes.

"Everyone, open your hymnals to page 546," the cantor told us. "The responsorial psalm will be 'The Lord is my shepherd; there is nothing shall I want.'" What I *wanted* was to hear these three little words: *"Mass is ended."*

Okay, I have a confession to make. I hated church. Not the institution. Just "church." The one-hour-every-Sunday-morning slice out of my day that most other folks refer to as "mass." Before you dismiss me as a horrible blasphemer and close this book, allow me to offer one extra bit of information. I was eight years old when this story took place.

Now grown up (and with an attention span far in excess of the five-minute limit I had in those days), I've grown to *love* church (the institution *and* the weekly gathering). The spiritual infusion has helped ground me as I mourn Mom's loss. And it helps me feel closer to her, as well. After all, Mom dragged me—sorry, *took* me—to church every week.

I remember that particular morning with a mix of warmth in my heart and tears in my eyes—as I tug on the silver-plated Fossil watch I snagged during a Black-Friday sale on Amazon.

I tell you this story for a reason—a reason that sparked a kind of personal epiphany. As I started my *good mourning* journey and began my research, I found that most of the mourning customs we use today were created in Ancient Rome. As in "Ancient Rome, the birthplace of Catholicism," the same religion that had the youthful me "trapped" in that church pew twenty-five years ago.

If I close my eyes, I can transport myself back there. I can smell the peppermint Tic Tac my mother had just eaten. I can remember the sternness of her "be-good-or-no-video-games" warning. I can even re-experience the boredom that induced the offending fidgeting in the first place.

When I realized we have been partaking in the same mourning customs for over two thousand years, I was bored all over again, which made me wonder…

- Did the Ancient Romans, the ones who wore dark-colored togas[4] for the rest of their lives after a loved one's death, pretend that putting on this distinctive garment helped them heal from their loss and move on?
- Did they tolerate being restricted from going to social gatherings for several months after the death of their family member?

---

4   Gill, N.S. "The Six Types of Togas Worn in Ancient Rome." Thoughtco. com, www.thoughtco.com/six-types-of-toga-in-ancient-rome-117805

- Did they really observe the "no laughter" ban?[5]

Obviously, we don't follow these prisoner-like rituals today. But the melancholic thinking has seeped into our brains. It still guides our mourning. We may not wear black every day.[6] But we reflect it because of those dark inner feelings.

And that's not a *good mourning*.

That holdover is a holdback. We can't seem to "get happy" again and perhaps even feel guilty about it if we do. This healing reticence manifests itself in subtle ways. Without even realizing why, we might avoid the latest comedy flick because the laughter the movie elicits might have others believe we're "over" our loss.

There's even a reluctance to fully mourn for fear of breaking some social norm. So we go through the motions, believing we're grieving in the "right" way, and in doing so follow a path that adds to our strife. We hold things in. And when we do that, problems arise—big ones.

Mental health professional Mandy Kloppers confirms that "long-term denial can lead to self-sabotage and an inability to know what is real and what is fabricated."[7] What a frightening

---

5   Hoyt, Alia. "How Grief Works." Science.howstuffworks.com, www.science.howstuffworks.com/life/grief1.htm

6   Kirk, Julie. "Death Rituals." Dying.lovetoknow.com, www.dying.lovetoknow.com/Death_Rituals

7   Kloppers, Mandy. "Too Much Pretending." Mentalhelp.net, www.mentalhelp.net/blogs/too-much-pretending/

thought. Looking back on my situation, I wonder where I'd be today had I pretended that all the grief practices—the grief counseling, the Facebook groups, the books, the over-sympathizing about my suddenly motherless life—were actually doing some good. Who knows? I do know for me it wouldn't be good.

Had I lived back in Roman times, I believe I'd be wearing that black straight-jacket—while sitting alone in a cold dark room for weeks, months, or even years. An outlook like that is even darker than the room I'd confined myself to.

We've traveled forward in time since then. But have our mourning practices advanced as far? My initial answer: Not in the slightest. I looked at our current-day culture and my notions about mourning were confirmed.

We *do* still wear black. We *do* still withdraw from our closest friends (at least for a while). We *do* stop dating. We *do* avoid our own partners and spouses. We *do* still follow our "ancestors"—the Romans. I was about to blame them for giving us and future generations these unimaginative, damaging, and downright lousy mourning practices they created.

That was, until I "met" Marcus Tullius Cicero.[8] He was one of Ancient Rome's most revered orators, politicians, and visionaries. I discovered the impetus of Cicero's own *good mourning*

---

8   "Dacre Balsdon, John P.V., and Ferguson, John. Marcus Tullius Cicero." Britannica.com, https://www.britannica.com/biography/Cicero

journey was the death of his daughter, Tullia[9] who died giving birth in 45 BC. He quickly became my hero because of what he did after his loss. I blew a kiss to the Heavens for granting the first of my *good mourning* epiphanies.

When I serendipitously stumbled upon an academic essay, *"Coping with Bereavement and Grief: Lessons from History,"* by Dr. Han Baltussen, a professor of classics from the University of Adelaide in Australia, I experienced an empathetic heartache for Cicero as I read of this poor man's loss.

Cicero *"had already lost his status as a politician and had recently been divorced,"* Prof. Baltussen wrote. *"The loss of his daughter tipped him over the edge and landed him in a depression. Cicero's method of coping, it transpires, was to engage in the 'healing arts' of reading and writing."*

This passage, in particular, spoke to me. Cicero *"not only wrote letters about setting up a monument but also about his reading activities, perusing every possible book about grief and consolation,"* the professor recounted. *"Unhappy about his findings, he decided to write his own consolation to himself."*

I read this passage over and over: *"Unhappy about his findings, he decided to write his own consolation to himself."*

Cicero himself seemed to have bewitched me, guiding me to click my own pair of ruby slippers like Dorothy in the Frank Baum family classic, *The Wonderful Wizard of Oz.* Reading

---

9   Tullia (daughter of Cicero). Wikipedia.org, www.en.wikipedia.org/wiki/
     Tullia_(daughter_of_Cicero)

of his journey of self-healing that was uncannily similar to my own, I finally realized—there's no place like "Rome."

Thanks to Cicero and his writings, Rome was now a place where my soul was understood and my *good mourning* journey invigorated. He simply realized the available material wasn't easing his pain. That's it. Cicero's next step granted me one of life's most valued, most comforting insights about death—human reactions to grief really do stand the test of time.

Whether you're an ancient Roman named Marcus Tullius Cicero or a thirty-three-year-old American woman who lives in a Baltimore suburb called Pasadena, you must accept the hand you've been dealt. And you must do what it takes for *your soul* to heal and recover from your loss.

Your soul—and your soul only.

Each healing plan is unique to the person that plan is serving. Cicero followed his intuition, just as I have, to write his own consolation—his personal how-to manual to guide him on his *good mourning* journey. And it worked.

"After four months, [Cicero] emerged from his acute grief and launched into a vigorous program of philosophical writings," Prof. Baltussen tells us. *"Thus, Cicero, author by nature and therapist by necessity, was able to lift himself out of his sorrow by doing what he did best: reading and writing. His adjustment of the process, creating a distinctly Roman consolation, was a marker of his character and cultural context."*

As the professor concluded, *"We should make the rich resources of our cultural capital (accrued over centuries) available to cater for the variety of grief experiences. The ancient past has much to offer for today. But the choice of appropriate method will remain a personal one."*[10]

I couldn't have said it better myself. We each have our own *good mourning* path to follow—our own journey to make. We can study what our ancestors have done for inspiration. We can use all or part of what we find or discard it completely. We owe it to ourselves, and to our well-being, to tailor those practices to our own needs.

The fact that you're reading this book is proof that you're channeling your inner Cicero, just as I have done. Be proud that you took this important first step. You've already started your own *good mourning* journey toward a future that's bright with healing and hope.

Your journey may be uncannily similar to mine. Or it could be completely different. What's important is to foster our own healing if we're to move on with our lives.

I know I don't want to wear black or dark-colored togas (even if they are slimming) to mourn my mother. I want to steal Joseph's technicolor dream coat and blow into one of those Alphorns, (the ones from the '90s Ricola cough drop

---

10 Baltussen, Han. "Coping with Bereavement and Grief: Lessons from History." Theconversation.com, www.theconversation.com/coping-with-bereavement-and-grief-lessons-from-history-9088

commercials), dressed in a Dirndl at the top of the Swiss Alps to show how much I love her.

While I may never get to do that (though I now see this as an EPIC idea, and have already added it to my personal bucket list), I am certain I'll continue to mourn one of the most amazing women ever in the way that serves me best. And you can do the same with your loved ones.

I'm not a priest, but I am declaring that the "mass is ended." The dark mass where our outlook on life is dominated by the deep blackness of loss. It's a dark world—one in which you fear the sun will never rise again.

But it will.

When you have a *good mourning*, that emotional dawn will come again. Just like it did for C.S. Lewis, another fellow *good mourning-er* I've come to admire as much as Cicero. In the next chapter, I'll tell you all about his journey.

GOOD MOURNING INSIGHTS

- Instead of blaming our ancestors for the definition of grief and mourning, we can learn from them.
- We can apply what we've learned from history or use it as a springboard into finding our own way on our *good mourning* journey.
- We don't have to mourn in any societal-prescribed way.
- We can write our own mourning practices.

CHAPTER 2

I LOVE LUCY

———

*"Lucy buried her head in his mane to hide
from his face. But there must have been some
magic in his mane. She could feel lion-strength
going into her. Quite suddenly she sat up. 'I'm
sorry, Aslan,' she said. 'I'm ready now.'*

*'Now you are a lioness,' said Aslan. 'And
now all Narnia will be renewed.'"*

—C.S. LEWIS,
THE CHRONICLES OF NARNIA: PRINCE CASPIAN

I've always been a creature of habit.

"Mom, can you put it on again?" I asked, hiding my smile (and
slight overbite) under the comforting brown, pink-and-tan
afghan. "Again, Jen?" my mother asked. "But we just watched
it."

She wasn't really surprised. After all, watching a movie over and over was a Hale family staple. My sisters Amanda and Becky did the same thing. "I know," I whispered. "But I really want to watch Lucy have tea and toast with Tumnus—again."

Mom sighed and gave in as she always did. The videotape, labeled *Lion, Witch and the Wardrobe* in my dad's script, went back into the VCR. She hit the rewind button and the movie whirred back to the beginning.

In a routine that left me feeling content and safe, Mom kissed my forehead, pried my favorite "Who's Hiding In My Mug?" cup from my grasp, and once again filled it with tea, milk, and a generous helping of sugar before heading up to the kitchen to replenish our teapot. As I drank it, the purple hippo (who lived inside) came out of his submerged hiding place, giving me an extra dollop of joy.

It was always the same. A few tea sips later, Mom came back down the carpeted steps and into the family room downstairs. She was balancing the familiar wooden tray, filled with another round of tea, sliced oranges and buttered toast she'd sprinkled with cinnamon sugar.

I was watching a favorite movie, drinking from my favorite mug and enjoying the warmth of that toasty afghan. All those things, coupled with my mother's presence—and those reassuring rituals she was just so wonderful with—reminded me that everything was right in my world. I was safe. And I was happy. I was seven years old.

Not long after my mother died in April 2018, I hit "rewind" and found myself watching this scene yet again. The catalyst for this revisitation was the C.S Lewis book, *A Grief Observed*, which I'd bought and read just after the funeral.

The purchase made sense at the time. After all, Lewis had comforted me so much as a child. I drew joy and reassurance from a fantasy tale featuring some of the most precious characters in all literature: a hospitable faun named Tumnus and a warrior lion named Aslan, all existing inside a mysterious wardrobe.

I was hoping, more expecting, that Lewis would do the same for me in his account of the loss of his wife Joy. Her tragic death came four short years after their 1956 marriage.[11] Looking for meaning and solace in every word—and somehow re-experiencing that warm sweetened tea of my youngest years—I read how he compared the premature death of his wife to a surgical amputation, an appropriate analogy for anyone navigating grief.

With the loss of my mother, I felt like the victim of a magic trick gone wrong—like the remaining half of one of those "saw-the-lady-in-two" displays, never to be made whole again.

Lewis' words hit home.

"Getting over [her death] so soon?" the author wrote. *"But the words are ambiguous. To say the patient is getting over it after*

11   Erickson, Angela. "14 Things You Probably Didn't Know about C.S. Lewis," Bookbub.com, www.bookbub.com/blog/facts-about-cs-lewis

an operation for appendicitis is one thing; after he's had his leg off is quite another. After that operation either the wounded stump heals or the man dies. If it heals, the fierce, continuous pain will stop. Presently he'll get back his strength and be able to stump about on his wooden leg. He has 'got over it.'"

But is having "got over it" the same as being truly healed? Lewis clearly had doubts.

"Though having recovered from the surgery, the patient will probably have recurrent pains in the stump all his life, and perhaps pretty bad ones; and he will always be a one-legged man," Lewis wrote. *"There will be hardly any moment when he forgets it. Bathing, dressing, sitting down and getting up again, even lying in bed, will all be different. His whole way of life will be changed. All sorts of pleasures and activities that he once took for granted will have to be simply written off. Duties too. At present, I am learning to get about on crutches. Perhaps I shall presently be given a wooden leg. But I shall never be a biped again."*[12]

I could relate. Like Lewis, I was left with a "disability" of the heart, mind, and soul, infirmities that were debilitating in their own inevitable way. My day-to-day duties were swallowed up in an apathetic quagmire. As for my long-term goals, my dreams of achievement, and plans I'd been making? They disappeared.

---

12   Lewis, C.S. "A Grief Observed Quotes." Goodreads.com, www.goodreads. com/work/quotes/894384-a-grief-observed

They were nowhere to be found. That's what the death of my mother had done to me. My reaction was an obvious one. I condemned C.S. Lewis. I wondered how someone as imaginative as he could offer such bleak, hopeless counsel.

That's the reality of death and loss, if we allow it to be so.

I'm not going to lie. I allowed Lewis' words to have that terrible effect on me. The ambitions, hopes, and upbeat dreams I'd once held for myself, and for my future, had disappeared, arm-in-arm with my mom's final breath.

It wasn't until I had the epiphany of all epiphanies—the one where I realized Cicero, the Ancient Roman who was guilty by association for giving us the worst set of mourning practices, was, in fact, the pioneer of the very first *good mourning* journey.

And second?

C.S. Lewis.

What I didn't realize was that *A Grief Observed* was Lewis' way of coping with his own grief. It was his "process." It was one valiant *good mourning* act—just like Cicero's written consolation.

I thought about re-reading *A Grief Observed*. Instead, I hit the rewind button, traveled back to my youth, and watched the Lewis-inspired *The Lion, the Witch and the Wardrobe*— just like in older, happier times. This time, I only re-watched it once. Because once is all it took to realize how much I loved

Lucy. No, not the zany redhead who entranced American audiences in the 1950s (though, I do love her, too). I'm talking about Lucy Pevensie from the *Chronicles* series.

When I was young, I loved Lucy's cute, colorful bows—and her dimples, too. As an adult, this affinity found a different, deeper target. I loved Lucy's fearlessness. I loved her ability to step courageously into the unknown land that lay within that eerie wardrobe. By taking that risk, Lucy allowed herself to quickly become the beacon against the darkness of the endless winter cast upon Narnia by the White Witch.

I couldn't help but wonder…

If I were faced with that same opportunity, could I demonstrate that same courage? Would I allow myself to be the light against the perpetual darkness of death? Could I do so now? I didn't know the answer. At least, not yet. But I realized I wanted to give it a try.

As I re-watched the movie and came to the scene where Lucy met Tumnus at the lamppost (a scene I'd always loved) something stirred deep within me. I thought back over all I had learned from Cicero and Lewis, including how they used reading and writing to cope with their grief. They validated everything I was feeling and more. But I still wasn't sure how to apply what I was thinking to what I was feeling—not exactly.

That's when I experienced yet another revelation. After consulting Grief.com, I discovered that the terms "grief" and "mourning," while used interchangeably in our lexicon, are in fact two totally different things.[13]

An obvious assessment, I know, but listen to this…

- Grief is what we feel on the *inside.*
- Mourning is what we experience and show to others on the *outside.*

In other words, grief is an emotion. Mourning is an action. This was energizing for me. I realized these observations were only a piece of the story. For me to actually start my *good mourning* journey, I had to experience and show my mourning to the world for one reason and one reason only—to heal my ailing heart.

Yes, this book you're holding right now is just the guide to help you set out on your own *good mourning* journey. It's up to you to go through with it. Trust me when I say: it's well worth the effort. I'm living proof, as are the sixteen fellow *good mourning-ers* in this book.

And so is Jennifer Coken, author of *When I Die, Take My Panties.* Just like my beloved Lucy, Jen put her feelings—and her words—into action. I'll tell you more about Jen's touching story in the next chapter.

First, let's do a quick recap of what we learned…

---

13   "Brief History of Grief and the Five Stages." Grief.com, www.grief.com/the-history/

GOOD MOURNING INSIGHTS

- Grief and mourning are two totally different things.
  - Grief is what you feel on the inside.
  - Mourning is what you experience and show to others on the outside.
- True healing comes from mourning.

CHAPTER 3

REBEL WITH A CAUSE

—

"You'll never plow a field by turning it over in your mind."

—IRISH PROVERB

I didn't really want to go. Not really. But I was going.

I was a Spanish major at a small Catholic school in Baltimore, College of Notre Dame, and I needed to go abroad for my degree. The school sisters recommended foreign language students go in their junior year. Maybe they thought our college jitters would have worn off by then.

Not mine. My jitters not only multiplied but manifested in irrational fears of airports, airplanes, and the luggage section at Macy's.

I had toyed with the idea of going to Mexico. However, I knew deep down my worrywart of a mother might actually have a nervous breakdown if I did. I chose an idyllic town just outside of Madrid, Spain. I nervously signed the registration papers and then secretly hoped August 23, 2006 would never arrive. But it did. There was no turning back.

My ticket was in hand and my two oversized, apple red suitcases were stuffed with four months of college clothes. There was one thing I didn't need to pack, but it was coming with me. It was my "something to prove," first to myself, but even more so to my mother.

"Jenny, I really don't feel comfortable with you going to Spain," she pleaded. "I just called Sister Lamy and told her that all study abroad programs should be canceled this semester. It's just too unsafe with all the bombings happening over in Europe."

"Mom, I appreciate your concern, but the bombing happened in London a year ago. That's like a thousand miles away from Spain. I'll be fine. I promise," I replied defiantly.

It was all a front.

The truth was... I was scared. Really scared.

I could never let her know that. I didn't want her to worry even more than she was already planning to. When it came time to say goodbye at the airport gate, I hugged Dad, Amanda, and Becky and told them how much I loved them. When I slowly turned to Mom, I cracked. She wiped away my tears and whispered in my ear, "You're going to be just fine, Jen. I promise."

"I love you, Mom," I said.

She couldn't say it back or else she'd crack, too.

To avoid a long, lingering goodbye, I let go of her warm embrace and never looked back. I couldn't let her see the deluge of tears pouring down my face. I boarded the flight with my fellow Spanish major and soon-to-be lifelong best friend, Tabatha. As I tried to get comfortable in the stiff, tight-fit seat, I instantly felt a change. I felt a palpable *"I'm going to be okay"* that left me feeling reinvigorated after the emotionally draining goodbye scene that took place minutes before.

I took out my compact and reapplied my blush-pink lip gloss. As I wiped away the dusty layer of foundation on the mirror, I looked deep into my own eyes. The fear faded away. I felt at peace with my decision to venture to the mysterious land of bullfights, sangria, and flamenco dancing.

Leading up to this moment, I was not the adventurous type— at all. This trip to Spain was a defining moment in my life. Most kids get tattoos to prove they're old enough to make their own decisions. I, the biggest, most dependent home-body there ever was, studied abroad. I'm not going to lie. I felt like a total badass—a rebel, if you will. I was leaving Baltimore a skittish college student and would soon return a cultured world traveler. I conquered my fear that day.

After settling into my dorm, I resorted to my old fearful ways. I took the bus to school, came right home, and stayed in most nights. I barely drank an ounce of sangria. I frequented

McDonald's for comfort. While I was devouring my fifteenth M&M McFlurry, I called an intervention on myself.

I realized I was greatly limiting my experience and succumbing to something I call "fear traps." I was in Spain, for goodness' sake. I should be living it up. Instead, I forced myself to live a *Groundhog Day* kind of life, doing the same things over and over because they were familiar and safe.

I saw I was missing out on joy by remaining in these self-imposed fear traps. I needed to change my thinking. I threw the half-melted McFlurry in the trash, walked straight over to the train station, bought a ticket to Madrid and spent the entire day there alone. When the train arrived, I wasn't sure what I would do, but it didn't matter. What mattered was that I had broken free.

I never felt more alive as I walked around the *El Prado* museum taking in famous paintings like *Las Meninas* that I had studied for years. I stopped in a café to eat the best churros of my life. This impromptu trip was the best thing I had ever done. It gave me the freedom to venture to all parts of Spain, as well as Ireland, while abroad.

After my mother's wake, I was reminded of my semester in Spain and all the hurdles I overcame as I looked down at my flowy Flamenco look-a-like red dress. I got in my car and glanced in my rearview mirror. The woman with puffy, blood-shot eyes staring back at me looked a lot like me. However, it wasn't the me I used to know. Was the rebel still in there?

I wasn't sure. What I did know was I had to change my thinking in order to find that adventurous risk-taker again. I had my work cut out for me. Scientists claim that 80 percent[14] of our thoughts are negative. I'm not a statistician, but I'd bet that percentage is closer to 99.9 for a person who is grieving. Because of the trauma we were inevitably faced with, we often find ourselves caught in grief traps. Sound familiar?

Similar to the fear traps I experienced in Spain, grief traps represent the way we can trap ourselves in our own grief. Not just because it's comfortable but because it's familiar. More often than not, we do it because our grief is all we have left of our loved ones.

I spent months in my own grief traps, desperately clinging to any trace I had left of my mother. I wallowed, cried, procrastinated, stagnated, and commiserated. While these emotionally driven activities served their purpose for a while as a way to process my loss, they seemed to do more damage than good.

Especially when you consider that most of the thoughts we have on any given day are also 95 percent repetitive.[15] That means I had 95 percent of the same exact negative thoughts over and over again after my mother died. The same ones that kept me trapped in my grief. The only thing I've found that can break this repetitive pattern is to take action. It

---

14   Verma, Prakhar. "Destroy Negativity from Your Mind with This Simple Exercise." Medium.com, www.medium.com/the-mission/a-practical-hack-to-combat-negative-thoughts-in-2-minutes-or-less-cc3d1bddb3af

15   Ibid

may appear simple on the surface but can be an ultra-healing experience.

While she's not a historical figure like Cicero or a world-famous author like C.S. Lewis (at least not yet), Jen Coken, the author of *When I Die, Take My Panties* and fellow *good mourning-er,* showed me the importance of taking action early on in my grief journey.

After a mutual friend heard of my mother's passing, she gave Jen my number. My dear friend, Jen, stood out to me because she quickly took action to introduce herself to me. Without any hesitation, she called me on my first motherless Mother's Day. Thinking she was a telemarketer, I didn't answer. That didn't deter her. She proceeded to leave me the longest, sweetest message possible, warmly welcoming me into what she referred to as the "unwanted sisterhood" of women who've lost their mothers to cancer. Jen lost her mother, Jan, in 2011 to ovarian cancer.

I immediately called Jen back and ordered her book. With every page, Jen quickly proved she was not only a rebel griever, but she was one *with* a cause. While each page beautifully documented the gradual yet heartbreaking loss of her mother, who was also her best friend, the book had a mission:

To help women all over the world prevent ovarian cancer—forever.

When I reached the end of the book, I was surprised to find a comprehensive list of warning signs for ovarian cancer, plus dozens of cancer resources. As a woman, I was touched.

But as a woman of action, I was inspired. The cogs in my mind were spinning. I wondered, *What can I do to help rid the world of cancer, too?* At first, I considered following Jen's lead and doing something similar for lung cancer prevention. Then, I had another idea. I felt called to create a group dedicated to showing people who are grieving how to mourn with joy.

It would be called *Good Mourning.*

While this new support group is still growing, its impact is big. We had a karaoke night to which a good friend who had lost both parents at a young age came. Afterward, she told me: "Jen, I have not laughed that hard in a long time." My heart was full and I was ready to take even more action to help others find joy on their *good mourning* journey. This group was the impetus for writing the book you're holding in your hands right now.

None of this, the group or the book, would have been possible had I not chosen to change my mindset around grief and mourning. Cicero and C.S. both helped me out in that department. They showed me that so much of our loss can be processed through reading and writing. Reading their stories and books helped me come to the conclusions I did.

Next, Jen Coken showed me the importance of taking action right away. But, most of all, Jen's book told me to pay attention to the valuable things that death can teach us about ourselves. The one thing I learned is that I am stronger than I thought. And, you are, too.

It's all thanks to something I call the *good mourning shift*. It's deep inside all of us but is dormant until we access it. I'll show you how to tap into the power of your own *good mourning shift* in the next chapter. Once you do, your life will change for the better.

But, first, here's a wrap-up of everything we've learned in part 1 so far...

GOOD MOURNING INSIGHTS

- Instead of blaming our ancestors for the definition of grief and mourning, we can learn from them.
- We can apply what we've learned from history or use it as a springboard into finding our own way on our *good mourning* journey.
- Grief is what you feel on the inside. Mourning is what you experience and show to others on the outside.
- True healing comes from mourning.
- Change your thoughts, take action, and begin the healing process.

PART 2

PRINCIPLES OF THE *GOOD MOURNING JOURNEY*

CHAPTER 4

SHIFTS HAPPEN

"Grief does not change you, Hazel. It reveals you."

—JOHN GREEN, *THE FAULT IN OUR STARS*

Everything was *always* in the same place in that store. Always.

As a kid, I could walk around Mom's go-to grocery store, Giant, with my eyes closed and never bump into a thing—not the three-tiered banana display nor the red delicious apple crate. I knew they sat right next to the trough of whole peanuts located just to the left of the tropical fruit section with the mainstay brown and white "2 for $1" coconuts sign.

The store's blueprint was ingrained in my ten-year-old brain. I could tell you the exact placement of every raisin, rutabaga, and box of Apple Jacks breakfast cereal. That last one was the only thing on my mind. Without fail, I snuck my favorite cereal into her cart when she wasn't looking. However, hiding the bright green box under a sack of potatoes was futile.

Without fail, my mom promptly put the sugary stowaway back on the shelf. Pouting did not help.

"Mom, can I pleeease get them this time?"

"No, Jen, I don't want you to get any more cavities this year."

I didn't care about my teeth. All I could think about was my stomach. I wasn't going to let my foiled "Operation Apple Jacks" mission get in the way of trying to score at least one thing I wanted. The next aisle held another snack goldmine filled with crackers, biscuits, and cookies. The Oreos were calling my name, and again my watchdog mom caught me red-handed, saying, "Jennifer, I am not going to tell you again. Put those back right now."

My mid-aisle foraging backfired. I had distracted her too much.

As my mother placed the items on the belt at the checkout line, she turned to me and said, "Jenny, I've gotta run back and grab oranges." That's when it hit me—the crippling fear that overcame me any time I lost sight of my mom. No matter how well I knew the ins and outs of that store—the store I had been to dozens of times before—I desperately needed to know exactly where she was at every moment.

"No, Mom, nooo," I pleaded as tears welled in my eyes.

She firmly grabbed my shoulders and crouched down to my level. "Jennifer, I am NOT going to leave you in this store."

All of a sudden, the lightbulb went off and my frightened, little-girl brain suddenly calmed. In that moment, I was finally freed from my lifelong struggle with intense separation anxiety. In Lane 7 at my mother's favorite grocery store, my soul shifted from dependent, scared child to independent young woman.

The truth is, shifts like this happen all the time. Sometimes we're in tune with them. Sometimes we're not. They can happen in our careers, relationships, and spiritual lives. They can even happen when we least expect them.

Barrie Davenport, a personal and career coach, wrote an article that discussed the idea of mind shifts. She believes two things must be present for mind shifts to happen. The first is awareness. She writes, "*Sometimes awareness hits us on the head like a brick, and our minds have to be cracked open. Big events like a job loss, relationship break-up or death can shock us into awareness and cause a mind shift.*"

That's exactly what happened to me in the grocery store that day. It was as if a brick fell from the ceiling and hit me on the head. I was awakened to the fact my mother was NOT going to leave me in that store, but even more, she was NOT going to leave me alone anywhere we went. This was a life-changing shift for me.

Unfortunately, she had to break her promise the morning she died.

This time, the awareness of this unfortunate event wasn't a brick that hit me in the head. It was a boulder that left a gaping hole in my heart and life. When I witnessed her breathe her final breath, a different mind shift occurred. Yet in this moment, the shift was regressive, leaving me paralyzed with sadness and fear. Most of all, it left me excruciatingly aware of my new motherless reality. I remember thinking as I lay next to her, gently rubbing her cold hand, *My life will never be the same again.*

It certainly hasn't been.

Not a minute goes by that I am not thinking, *My mother can't really be gone.* The woman who gave birth to me, raised me, nurtured me, and loved me when no one else did is gone from this earth, never to return. This mind-numbing reality hasn't faded, at least not yet.

Davenport believes timing also plays a role in the occurrence of mind shifts. She continued, "*Sometimes the circumstances in our lives make [shifts] possible. Occasionally the timing is so absolutely ripe for a shift that it's virtually inevitable. It descends on us like grace. All things are in alignment for the pieces to fall into place.*"

The timing of this shift was inevitable. I didn't have a choice in the matter of my mother's premature death. If I did, you wouldn't be reading this book right now. These mind shifts can show up unannounced—and we can be aware they're there—but it's ultimately up to us to tap into their power.

"*A mind shift is a change of focus and perception. It can have extraordinary power to make relationships more positive and healthy; to improve your focus and rate of success; and to build self-esteem and overall happiness. A mind shift is an 'ah ha' moment on steroids. It's the movement of the tectonic plates in your psyche, opening your mind to entirely new ways of thinking and acting,"* Davenport concluded.[16]

The tectonic plates moved in my psyche almost immediately, making room for new ways of thinking and acting after my mother's death. Most of all, this shift made room for my inner strength to shine as it had never shone before. By allowing the power of this shift to take over, the intense wave of fear and sadness I experienced the moment my mother died started to fade away.

My tears stopped flowing and my mind was clear for the first time since before she was diagnosed with cancer. As strange as it may sound, I was even at peace with her being gone, which felt so foreign to me, considering my dependence on her for most of my life.

All of this could only be explained by an ultra-specific mind shift that's deep inside all of us but remains dormant until we access it. I call it the *good mourning shift.* Mine showed up with a vengeance that late April morning when I was forced to say goodbye to the most amazing woman I'll ever know. What I'm about to tell you still boggles my mind but is evidence that the power of the *good mourning shift* is beyond our own understanding.

---

16   Davenport, Barrie. "10 Life-Altering Mind Shifts to Rock Your World." Pickthebrain.com, www.pickthebrain.com/blog/10-life-altering-mind-shifts-to-rock-your-world/

After my family dispersed to try to get some rest, I stayed in the room alone with my deceased mother. In that moment, I knew something about me was different. As a child, I was always petrified to go to viewings at funeral homes, let alone be the only person in the room with a dead body. This time, I wasn't afraid. It was as if this *good mourning shift* made me fearless.

As my mother lay there completely still with her lips pursed in the form of a tiny smile—one I believe she cracked once she saw who was greeting her at heaven's gate—I couldn't take my eyes off of her. For hours, I just stared at her, trying desperately to imprint her beautiful face in my memory forever.

When one of the hospice nurses showed up at 3:30 a.m. to pronounce my mother officially dead, I didn't flinch. Though seeing her full name, Suzanne Maria Hale, on the death certificate was surreal, I knew the real Sue Hale would never leave her family behind. I knew deep down her death wasn't the end for me. It certainly wasn't the end for her, either. As the nurse tucked her body in one final time, it was as if her spirit whispered in my ear, "I'll never leave you," just like she did in the grocery store. I believed her then, so why would this time be any different?

After the nurse left, I continued to wait with my mother. As she lay peacefully on her own bed's lovely white eyelet comforter, I sat on the adjacent hospital bed. She had cursed it for being dreadfully uncomfortable. She was right, like always. It was stiff as a board, but it gave me a clear shot of her bureau.

There in a dusty frame was the photo from my First Holy Communion, where I wore a white veil and cheesy grin. I stood proudly between my two sisters, Becky and Amanda, perfect placement since I was the middle daughter. I hated that picture because it showed the beginning of my portly adolescent figure. Regardless of what I thought, it had been a mainstay on her dresser for twenty-five years, a true testament to her unconditional love of my chubby cheeks.

A sudden knock on the front door broke my reverie. My father, Jeff, got up from resting on the living room sofa to answer it. He invited in the two gracious representatives from the funeral home. They respectfully asked me to leave the room as they prepared Mom's body for her final departure from our family home.

I never would've dreamed I'd have the strength to watch her be carried out our front door, but I did. It was only possible thanks to this mysterious *good mourning shift*. After my mother's body was driven down our long, winding driveway for the last time, I gave Dad the biggest, longest, most genuine hug of my life. He returned it with just as much passion. Once we let go of each other, he gave me one of his signature winks and adjourned to the sofa.

I returned to my mom's room, a room that will forever have significance in my life. From a haven for me and my toys when I was a kid to a sacred temple where I go to reflect on my mother's eternal love for me, this room is now a part of me. It's where my *good mourning shift* officially began.

Now, it's time to tap into your own.

If you're a little skeptical about this "shift," I completely understand. It does seem strange to think we all have this inner resilience ready to use when we're forced to deal with a significant loss in our lives. Regardless if you believe this *good mourning shift* exists or not, you can tap into your own inner strength, and your life can shift for the better.

This *good mourning shift* allows us to change the way we look at, feel about, and react to the painful, new void in our lives. It reminds us how strong we really are, giving us the chance to heal, grow, and transform ourselves from the inside out. This shift can help us yield beautiful things in our lives including new friendships, new experiences, new challenges, and most of all, a new you. Once you envision all the goodness that can come after your loss, you will begin to have a *good mourning*.

Since Mom died, I have discovered her boundless love isn't contained to her eleven-by-fourteen bedroom where I last felt it. Thanks to tapping into my own *good mourning shift*, I can find her love everywhere I go. To see, feel, or taste it, all I have to do is ask. Sometimes I don't have to. My mother's spirit often shows up just like the sun appears in the bright blue sky every single morning.

It's really no surprise because she was a tried-and-true morning person, after all. The moment her alarm clock rattled in her ear, she was up. After brushing her teeth, she'd head into the kitchen to brew a pot of coffee and then take her sweet dog for a walk around the tree farm. My mom was ready to conquer the world before I lifted my head off my pillow.

While I never was nor ever will be a morning person, I will forever be a *good mourning* person. I view every day as an opportunity to celebrate the one-of-a-kind mother I had by living my absolute best life possible. Is it always easy? No, it's not. I have shifted back many times, succumbing to my own grief traps. That's why I've put together these ideas to keep me on track each morning. I'll share them with you in the next chapter.

Before we get there, here's what we learned...

GOOD MOURNING INSIGHTS

- Mind shifts happen all the time. It takes awareness, timing, and willingness to act to make the most use of them.
- The *good mourning shift* paves the way for you to heal, grow, and transform your life after your loved one's death.
- Once you tap into your own *good mourning shift*, your life will change for the better.

CHAPTER 5

MOURNING ROUTINE

"The early bird catcheth the worm."

—ENGLISH PROVERB

I was always running late.

As a young girl, I'd stay in my white cast iron bed until the last possible second. When Mom came into my room, I'd burrow down under my puffy comforter and play possum. That was my game to avoid starting my day, every day.

Mom was a better player than me. Not just at possum but at mastering the whole "morning routine" thing. Her first move was to pull my hair back and whisper in my ear, "Jenny, it's time to get up." That was my cue to roll over and pretend to be asleep. Meanwhile, she curated a perfectly coordinated outfit with a matching hair scrunchie for me. Then she left. After about ten minutes, which felt like ten seconds to me, she came back to pull up the shades. That's when the sun beamed straight into my eyes. Still, that wasn't enough to rouse me.

My mother was strategic.

In order to officially interrupt my grizzly bear slumber, she had to pull out the winning move.

The washcloth.

This devil rag was the bane of my existence. The high-pitched squeal it made as she dragged it across the dewy window was like nails on a chalkboard to me. Damn, she was good. After just one insufferable swipe, I was up, and the score was tallied.

Mom–1.

Jen–0.

With only fifteen minutes to get dressed, eat breakfast, and run down our long driveway to the bus, I was in a panic. I sprinted to the bathroom, brushed my teeth, threw on the navy-blue USA sweater, jeans, and black tennis shoes Mom had carefully placed at the foot of my bed, grabbed my book-bag, and bolted up the stairs and into the kitchen. "Mom, can you put this in my hair?" As I handed her the red hair tie that perfectly matched the flag's stripes on my sweater, I noticed the chocolate Ovaltine, stirred and ready, along with my favorite cinnamon toaster waffles. My lunch was made, too. I had no doubt there was ice cream money and a sweet note inside.

Then, I saw it—my least favorite part of my dreaded morning routine. My vitamin.

This wasn't an ordinary vitamin. It was a tiny, chalky, chemical-tasting pill in the shape of Fred Flintstone. While Mom wasn't looking, I hid ole Fred behind the basket where the car keys were kept.

"How's that, Jen?" she asked.

"Mooommm, I like it tight! Can you please redo it?"

Keeping her frustration and comments to herself, she pulled my ponytail out and re-did it. "There, that's as tight as I can get it."

Being the contrarian I was in the morning, I ran to check it out in the mirror. "It's fine!" I yelled.

"You've gotta hurry, Jen. Amanda and Becky are already down by the bus stop," she exclaimed.

"Okay, I gotta go!" I ran to the front door, thinking I was in the clear.

Then I heard the worst words, "Jenny, wait! You forgot your vitamin!"

Yabba Dabba—Darn it!

I ran back to grab it, and her score advanced once again. "Let me see you put it in your mouth," she demanded.

I reluctantly placed this foul-tasting orange grenade on my tongue to appease her and ran out the door. I could not wait to get rid of it. When I reached the lamppost, I did my usual "spit and run" into the bush and skipped down the driveway.

The mystery of the multicolored shrub was detected later that summer as she tended to her monthly trimming. Though Mom was furious with me, I was quite proud of my work. Most of all, I had made the comeback I needed to even the score.

Mom–2.

Jen–2.

Back then, my mornings were always a struggle. When I reached high school, my routine got even messier, but my patient mom was always there to help me out the door. Mornings were her time to shine.

So, on April 25, 2018 when her beautiful spirit left her body, it was no surprise to me that she departed in the wee hours of the morning. That's when she began her new routine— watching over all she loved from above.

I also began mine. The problem was my mornings were in total disarray when she was alive. Even as a grown woman, I struggled with getting up and out the door in a timely fashion. How on God's green earth was I—the worst morning person of all—going to survive after my mother was gone?

At first, it wasn't pretty.

Though I was fully aware of my own *good mourning shift* and the power it gave me, I still had mornings when my grief took over. Some days, I felt sad and it hurt to move. My eyes would be swollen from crying myself to sleep the previous night. I even struggled to get up and it took every ounce of strength to pry myself out of bed.

Because of these mornings, I tried to formulate a new routine. At first, I couldn't get anything to stick. I'd get up and go for a run and eat a healthy breakfast one day. The next I'd sleep in and grab coffee and a donut to go. I even played possum just like when I was a kid. This time, I didn't have my mother there to play with me. I knew deep down in my soul I had to do something. My survival depended on it.

One morning, this headline from *The Daily Stoic* hit my inbox: "*A Good Morning Creates a Good Life.*" It began, "*The Stoics believed in the power of ritual, particularly at the beginning and the end of the day. For them, routines and rituals were not productivity hacks, but ways of living. In a world where so much was out of their control, committing to a practice they did control was a way of establishing and reminding themselves of their own power.* It was about *preparation. It was about creating peace.*" This passage spoke to me because my mother's death was certainly out of my control—like the death of your loved one was for you.

This columnist had interviewed Amy Landino, author of *Good Morning, Good Life.* "*A [book] title whose essence the Stoics would have likely agreed with. If you can win the morning, you can win the day,*" the writer commented.

Landino provides readers with three keys to a good morning, no matter what circumstances one is presented with. She suggests engaging the three steps of Movement, Mindfulness, and Mastery. In movement, the author says to *"Do something to move your body."* It can be ambitious, like going to the gym, or as simple as ten minutes of relaxed stretching or self-massage. Moving your body helps you wake up.

With mindfulness, Landino comments that *"It's too easy to pick up the phone or turn the TV on when you don't have anything else to do."* She suggests starting with a practice of something like meditation that helps people generate their own thoughts. She also suggests journaling.

Of mastery, she says, *"This one is my favorite because if not for my mastery time, I wouldn't have been able to figure out how to start my own business while I still had a full-time job ten years ago. Focus on something that you've been meaning to get around to or that you're passionate about."*[17]

The focus Landino places on the mind, body, and creativity is crucial to having a good morning. As the author of a different kind of "good morning" book, I'd like to add another "M" to the mix.

Mourning.

From my experience, the best thing to help you have a *good mourning* every day is to fuel your soul. You may wake up

---

17   "Good Morning, Good Life: An Interview With Amy Landino." Daily-stoic.com, www.dailystoic.com/amy-landino-interview/

to an alarm song like Bob Seger's "Old Time Rock and Roll" and do a little boogie on your way to the bathroom. Or you may watch a fifteen-minute snippet of a *Golden Girls* re-run.

My mourning routine includes taking a Flintstone vitamin (and actually eating it), singing "Supercalifragilisticexpialidocious" in the shower and creating an ultra-silly talking animal video using an app called *"My Talking Pet."*

I'll be forever grateful to a friend for introducing me to this pure amazingness. I select an animal like a koala bear and record a goofy message by putting words in its furry little mouth. I play it back afterward so I can have a good hearty chuckle that I feel in the depths of my soul.

Some days, I make these videos for my enjoyment only. Other days, I send them to my friends and family. My dad sent one of the most epic responses ever: *You need help.* I knew it had made him laugh, and that made me laugh even more!

If dancing, singing, or laughing isn't your thing, here's a list of other ideas to add to your *mourning* routine:

1. Volunteer at a local shelter or nonprofit organization
2. Perform a random act of kindness, e.g., buy the person's coffee behind you in the drive-through line
3. Go on a long, invigorating hike at a state park
4. Visit camels at your local zoo
5. Take your pug for a walk
6. Schedule a coffee date with your friend or college professor
7. Read old letters from your lost loved one
8. Go to a nearby pond or lake and sit for a while

9. Paint, sculpt, or paper-mâché a peacock
10. Bake chocolate and banana muffins

All of these practices may seem simple or even bizarre, but any one of them can help ground you on your *good mourning* journey. Once your soul is fed, you'll be able to carry out your day and your life with greater ease. You may gain a purpose or regain a passion.

In the next chapter, I'll show you step by step how to start your *good mourning* journey off on the right track. If you ever lose your way, I've provided you with your own roadmap.

Real quick, before we officially get started, here's what we learned from this chapter…

GOOD MOURNING INSIGHTS
- Morning routines help us regain control of our new lives without our loved ones.
- Mind, Movement, Mastery, AND Mourning all make up a good morning.
- Choosing one "mourning" activity each morning can fuel your soul and your life.

CHAPTER 6

THE ROAD
TO GREATNESS

———

*"Practice yourself, for heaven's sake in little
things, and then proceed to greater."*

—EPICTETUS

I didn't have a *normal* first crush.

Most little girls swoon over the little boys in their classes. Not
me. I only had eyes for one guy. He had thick brown locks
with an enviable side part. He wore over-sized, square glasses
and olive-green suits with matching ties.

I only saw him on Sunday afternoons. At 2 p.m. on the dot,
Mom would yell to me from the living room, "Jenny, it's your
boyfriend!" My heart would jump in my throat. I looked
forward to seeing him all week, but when it came time to
actually face him, I couldn't.

I had to wait until I heard him play.

The moment he pressed his lips against the reed in the black mouthpiece, all bets were off. I'd make my way out of my bedroom to get a closer look. I was mesmerized as he swayed from side to side with his eyes closed, creating the most beautiful music ever with the instrument he was born to play.

This mystery man was Henry Cuesta, the resident clarinetist on *The Lawrence Welk Show.*

While Mom enjoyed the show tunes and polkas of yesteryear, all I wanted was for my beau to serenade me with his rendition of "Stranger on the Shore." Henry Cuesta wasn't what you'd call a looker. He was an average-looking man from Corpus Christi, Texas. What made him special was the one thing we had in common—the clarinet.

I had wanted to be a trumpet player. I fantasized about pressing the three brass valves and playing the solemn "Taps" at girl scout camp. All of that went out the window when Mom placed a small, plastic case containing my musical fate in front of me.

When I saw my very own clarinet inside, I changed my tune. It seemed I was born to play the clarinet, like Henry. As a typical fourth grader, I had an affinity for naming all my possessions, so it was only natural for me to name my clarinet. Francesca, for some odd reason, was the name that came to me. It stuck, and she was all mine forever.

I adjoined each piece of my new best friend like a musical puzzle. In band class, I felt like a natural-born player like my beloved Henry. My skills, however, weren't those of a natural at all, unless the goal was to sound like a groundhog in heat. I even had trouble remembering simple rules like the open note "G" was played by blowing into the horn without pressing any keys.

I had my work cut out for me. Our band teacher warned us that the next three months before the Christmas concert were going to be grueling. I would have to practice every single night. It wouldn't be pretty, but I had to turn my weasel mating calls into music.

The moment I came home from school, I sat in the spare bedroom downstairs with my drill and scale sheets on the wooden stand Dad made for my sisters and me. I practiced until my amateur lips went numb. I was so focused on getting the notes right, I didn't realize when Mom snuck in behind me one night to tell me dinner was ready. She startled me, causing my clarinet to let out a big *"Squeeeaaak!"*

Mom couldn't help but snicker at the obnoxious blast that bellowed from the bell of Francesca's long, black horn. I quickly ducked down to wrestle in my case as a way to hide my beet-red face. Mom bit her lip to hide her laughter, then said, "It's dinnertime, Jen."

"Okay, Mom, I'll be right up," I mustered through my embarrassment.

After the squeak incident, I'd have flashbacks of Mom laughing at me every time I sat down to play. It was hard to overcome, but I was on a mission: "Jingle Bells" wasn't going to play itself. I tired of playing it over and over, but I couldn't quit. Like it or not, the concert would be here before I knew it, just like that "one-horse open sleigh."

The night of the Christmas recital finally arrived. I sat in the front row wearing my white button-down shirt and black pencil skirt. Like a cat licking its fur, I prepped my reed to perfection. Suddenly, the band teacher cued the clarinet section to play the intro. My mouth was shaking, and when I puffed air into my instrument, the worst possible thing happened. I had practiced and done everything in my power to prevent it, yet…

I squeaked.

This wasn't just any squeak. It was so loud the vibrations ricocheted off the concrete walls in the gymnasium like a cartload of monkeys fighting over a banana. I glanced into the audience and saw Mom laughing at my very public musical blunder, and I wanted to disappear off the face of the earth. I could easily have let that one incident stop me from ever playing the clarinet again. But I didn't.

In that moment, a fire was lit inside me. I promised I never, ever would experience a humiliating event like that again. I became religious about practicing for years because of that concert. My clarinet skills became so fine-tuned that I felt like the equivalent of a pre-teen Henry Cuesta.

I tell you this silly story now because it rings true for the death in our lives. Our new circumstances were handed to us, just like the clarinet was handed to me when my mom placed it, instead of a trumpet, in front of me that fateful day. At first, I didn't want it. I didn't think I could be any good at it. That didn't stop me. I picked the clarinet up and started to play it. It took practice at first, but I eventually made music.

Our *good mourning* journey is no different. Death can make or break us. You can use this unfortunate event as a time to shine or not. If you're so bold, you can choose the art of practice. This means doing something that helps you become better at mourning every single day. You may find it's easier to include a little joy if you stay on track with practice.

Farnoosh Brock, the author of *The Serving Mindset* and founder of Prolific Living, notes practice deserves recognition in her article, "Give Practice Some Glory."

She writes, *"Practice makes things possible. Practice opens doors but only—and not a minute sooner than—when you are ready for it. Consistent and regular practice has more of an exponential than a linear effect. If you practice your dance weekly, you advance very slowly over time, but if you practice it daily, the jump is not linear. It is exponential—in other words, it's a big jump, a huge jump, the kind of jump that makes the difference between good and great, mediocre and magnificent.*

"And practice rewards handsomely in all instances. It does not care about the state of economy, your business or even your relationships. When you practice something—anything—you

improve, you grow, you advance, you gain a skill and heaps of confidence to boot."

After soaking up her sentiments on practice, I came to the sobering reality that the last time I really gave something my all was my clarinet-playing days. Though I had trained to become a swimmer in high school and a long-distance runner in my late twenties, neither compared to the kind of dedication I poured into mastering the clarinet.

My daily practice led to an exponential jump into greatness when I became a member of the All-County Band in eighth grade. As Brock so eloquently put it, *"I improved, I grew, I advanced, I gained a new skill and heaps of confidence to boot."* That happened when I committed myself to the daily practice of playing the clarinet.

I now exercise that same level of dedication to the daily practice of mourning my mother's loss. I strive to *"improve, to grow, to advance, to gain a new skill and heaps of confidence"* on my *good mourning* journey. Because when I do, it is like my mother never left. Through these practices, she's still present in my life. I'm able to celebrate, laugh, and spend time as if I were with her every single day.

Brock concluded, *"Practice is tangible. Motivation and inspiration are sometimes fleeting but practice, you can hold on to it. You can count on it. You can schedule it. You can plan it. You can commit to it. You can return to it anytime so long as you believe in its power and its rewards.*

"So whatever your goals, your desirable skills, your artistic aspirations and dreams of creativity, build a consistent, unshakable practice around it. Stay the course, detach from the end-goal and delve into the world and wonder of your practice.

"Fall in love with the slow, the steady, and after a while, the significant progress which awaits you. Fall in love with your practice and compromise it for nothing in exchange on your path to greatness."[18]

Starting with a set of daily *good mourning* practices, you can create a path to greatness. I've paired each of the letters of the phrase *"Have a Good Mourning"* with a daily practice for you to find joy again and grow from your loss.

Here they are...

- **H**appiness: Find the one thing that gives you the most joy and hold onto it.
- **A**ction: Do something that helps others but also makes you feel great.
- **V**ictory: Celebrate big and small achievements every single day.
- **E**xpression: Speak your truth.
- **A**lliance: Find a supportive community that pushes you as you grow.
- **G**enerosity: Do something nice for others as often as you can.

---

18 Brock, Farnoosh. "The Importance of Practice: Use it or Lost it. Prolificliving.com, www.prolificliving.com/the-importance-of-practice-use-it-or-lose-it/

- **O**penness: Open your eyes to possibilities that your loved one is nearby.
- **O**riginality: Find the thing that makes you "tick" and explore the possibilities.
- **D**etermination: Persevere no matter what.
- **M**emories: Keep your memories close to your heart as you bring them to life.
- **O**smosis: Share your loved one's gifts with the world.
- **U**niqueness: Forge a brand-new life path, if you so choose.
- **R**ituals: Allot time to celebrate your loved one.
- **N**ostalgia: Relive the fun times from your past.
- **I**nvention: Recreate a new you from the inside out.
- **N**urturing: Find healing in your caring for others.
- **G**reatness: Realize you're *much* stronger than you think.

If one sounds interesting to you, just flip straight to the chapter. Each story stands on its own. I'll introduce you to a fellow *good mourning-er* who's traveled their own path and shared what they got from their journey.

In the next chapter, you'll learn how my sisters and I bonded with Mom over our love of dogs. We'll also visit with Polly-anna and her story and my wild love of something unusual. We'll look at happiness and ways to choose it.

But first, here's a wrap-up of everything we've learned in part 2...

GOOD MOURNING INSIGHTS
- Mind shifts happen all the time. It takes awareness, timing, and willingness to act to make the most use of them.

- The *good mourning shift* paves way for you to heal, grow, and transform your life after your loved one's death.
- Once you tap into your own *good mourning shift*, your life will change for the better.
- Morning routines help us regain control of our new lives without our loved ones.
- Mind, Movement, Mastery, AND Mourning all make up a *good morning*.
- Choosing one "mourning" activity each morning can fuel your soul and your life.
- The art of daily practice leads to greatness on your *good mourning* journey.
- There is no "one size fits all" when it comes to mourning.
- Pick and choose the *good mourning* practices that suit your needs and desires at any point on your journey.

PART 3

THE *GOOD MOURNING* ROADMAP

CHAPTER 7

HAPPINESS—JEN'S LOVE RUNS SHEEP

———

"It's a helluva start, being able to recognize what makes you happy."

—LUCILLE BALL

When it snowed, the trees were never safe.

Never.

My sisters and I did our best to dodge the fir seedlings Dad planted the spring before. They were little green landmines that our innertubes flattened like pancakes. With fewer obstacles in our path, our sleds compacted the snow into a slick track, making rides down the long hill in front of our house exhilarating and fun. At the end, we'd lie in the snow and listen to the quiet, catching our breath.

The wistful silence of the snowy afternoon was broken by Mom, who flung the kitchen window open to draw our attention to the slow-moving black object in the distance, "Girls, look, there's Night!" Normally, we'd be alarmed to see our furry friend on the road, but the mounds of early-December snow had made it impassable to cars. He was completely safe as he made his trek down the slippery street.

Night veered onto our long driveway as if he had put on a left turn signal. We stopped our snow fun to watch him cantor up the hill. He had a stride that would make any appaloosa jealous. What made his gait so special was the fact that this black lab had only three legs.

His tripod stance didn't give him the opportunity to run like his canine cohorts. We believed his owner had abandoned him because of his missing leg and left him to fend for himself and find food where he could. Mom always had dog food on hand, and she made sure Night felt welcome when he visited.

My sisters and I rushed to greet Night when his snow-covered nose reached the lamppost. We plopped down on padded knees right in front of him, and no matter how wet or cold or smelly he was, we planted kisses on top of his dirty head. We couldn't help but shower Night with love. Neither could Mom. Not two minutes passed before she was on the front porch with his usual spread—an old Tupperware lid topped with a glob of wet dog food, two uncooked hotdogs, three slices of cheddar cheese and a handful of bone-shaped treats. Night devoured it all.

"Mom, can we adopt Night?" we asked.

"I'd love to, girls, but Night is a free spirit. He goes as the wind blows."

Our faces dropped with disappointment. She knew giving the vagabond dog a couple of cheap hotdogs wasn't going to cut it much longer. Mom knew what to do.

Christmas finally arrived. We tore through our perfect piles of ultra-thoughtful gifts "Santa" displayed the night before. Mom came downstairs to see our progress, carrying her coffee in one hand and an extra present she had saved for last in the other. She called us over to her chair and placed the lone box in front of us. Greedily, we ripped open the mystery box and a high-pitched clink resounded from the metal clasp of a leash hitting the tin dog bowl.

We screamed in unison as I read the note tucked inside, "On March 1st, we will be welcoming a new addition to our family. A black lab puppy."

We threw our arms around Mom's neck for the best group hug ever.

"Margie's black lab, Hershey, just had puppies. I want you girls to come with me to pick one out," Mom said.

Our eyes lit up like fireworks. "We're getting a dog!" We jumped up and down with excitement.

"Any idea what you want to name her?" Mom polled us kids.

"I think we should get a girl and name her Missy after your dog, Mom," I piped up. Our dream of becoming official dog owners finally came true, making this our favorite "Christ-miss" ever. We picked Missy out and brought her home. For much of our childhood, she held a special place in all our hearts. Some are born dog people—and it was in our blood.

We each got the "unconditional dog-loving gene" from Mom's DNA. Naturally, we gravitated toward Night, the first dog to come on our property. With him, we had an intermittent, surface-level kind of love. It was in full bloom when he visited but would sadly dissipate when he left. That's when Mom recognized she wanted us to have a mainstay dog with which we could develop a deep-rooted love that fed our souls every day. That was Missy.

Mom was always so good at seeing what made the people around her happy. Her natural instincts blessed my sisters and me many times over. She would surprise us with things like a dog, a stuffed animal when we got sick, or even a dress for an upcoming dance. When she died, we had to teach ourselves how to read our own happiness meters again. Because only then could they help lead us to the healing we so desperately desired.

After Mom was gone, I yearned for that same dog connection we once shared. Little did I know the "dogs" in my future would be big, white, and wooly and go by the names of Big Ben, Buttons, and Lady Baa Baa. The moment I unlocked the barn gate at Kinder Farm Park for my first duty as a genuine sheep feeder, I had butterflies in my stomach. I hoped they would like me. When we locked eyes, our hearts locked, too. I was hopelessly smitten with my new friends.

Once the farmer, Roy, showed me where the food was and told me exactly how much to give them, I couldn't wait to get started. As I filled the bucket, I watched Roy interact with each sheep. He gave Big Ben a tough scratch on the head while he sweet-talked Buttons. I wanted a connection for myself, but I knew it would take more than just feeding them on Friday mornings to get it. That's when I made a commitment to be the best feeder—and best friend—I could be to these sheep.

The overwhelming satisfaction I get visiting and feeding my sheep friends every week is immeasurable. When I leave the barn, I am always on a sheep high, if that's even a thing. Thinking of their motor mouths chewing their food makes me smile. I am even one of those annoying sheep moms, showing pictures of my "babies" to my friends and family every chance I get. I can't help it. Sharing the boundless joy they give me with everyone I encounter makes me very happy.

If you're wondering, *What kinds of things make* me *happy?* but have no clue where to begin, I'd like to introduce you to a dear friend of mine. Her name is Pollyanna. She's the brainchild of author Eleanor H. Porter who was later brought to life in a Disney movie from 1960. This film has to be one of my favorites of all time.

On the surface Pollyanna was perfect. Perfect blond hair, perfect blue eyes, perfect disposition. In reality, her life was far from perfect. She lost both of her parents and was sent to live with her aristocratic, snooty Aunt Polly in the town of Harrington.

Before her father died, he gave Pollyanna one of the best gifts he could have. He taught her how to play the "glad game." The object was to find something to be happy about no matter the circumstance. She'd play it with everyone in Harrington, including the hermit Mr. Pendergast and the hypochondriac Mrs. Snow. She had the whole town so love-drunk with her affinity for life and happiness that they adopted her mindset. Even her cold-hearted aunt joined in.

Then the tables were turned. Pollyanna fell from her balcony window and lost her ability to walk. Her friend challenged her to play the glad game, and she refused. She couldn't for the life of her figure out what she could possibly be happy about. It wasn't until hundreds of people, who had seen the gladness light because of Pollyanna, showered her with love that she found her reason to be happy again.

When we lose someone we care deeply about, it's hard—I mean really, really hard—to find something to be happy about. When I lost Mom, I was just as distraught as Polly-anna. I could still physically walk, but I didn't know how to put one foot in front of the other on this new path without her. The sobering reality of Mom's absence from every future moment of my life tripped me up. It was mind-numbing.

I had two choices.

1. Allow my new motherless circumstances to completely ruin every possible chance of happiness that came my way, or…
2. Choose happiness.

I chose happiness.

This new mindset didn't come naturally for me. Even so, I was not deterred from pursuing happiness in some way, shape, or form every day. I do it now because my mother would want me to be happy. Most of all, I want to honor Mom and all she sacrificed to raise our family. She raised me to be a strong, independent woman who could create happiness in the midst of a storm.

If you've just begun your *good mourning* journey, your search for happiness may seem daunting. You could look everywhere and not see a sign. I promise, if you keep an open mind, your happiness will hit you when you least expect it, like me with my sheep friends. I was attracted to them like white on fleece. Because of this love, I'm now drawn to even more eccentric animal connections.

For instance, I was at the county farm fair last summer, and when I turned the corner, there was Sam—a 1,600-pound, tan creature with a hump. This camel had a big heart and a strong back to allow a grown woman like me to sit directly on his hump for a short tour around the field. I was in awe at how much my ride atop this massive Arabian wonder made me smile from ear to ear.

If I hadn't opened up to happiness in that moment, I would never have imagined myself owning a camel farm one day. Yes, I actually had that thought. Whether I liked it or not, camels made me happy. The only problem is they're twenty thousand dollars apiece. I'm going to have to sell a lot of books to buy just one of these lumpy nomads (so tell your friends)!

I can't deny I've been thinking about Sam ever since that wonderful day. I often think to myself (because I can't say this aloud and still be considered sane) *Could I actually own a camel ranch one day?* Only time will tell. No matter how weird it is to entertain, I continue to explore this idea because it makes me happy.

I've found the key to thriving on the *good mourning* journey is to first choose happiness. It's not easy. You may need to start by playing the glad game like Pollyanna. You will find at least something, even if it's small, that makes you happy despite your circumstances. For Pollyanna, it was getting well so she could return to her family in Harrington. For me, it is feeding my fleecy friends and riding Sam the camel.

When we tap into what makes us happy right now, our lives start to open up. We see things we didn't see before. Seeking happiness every day awakens us to what really matters. That's when we know we'll be okay. Our loved ones wouldn't want it any other way.

In the next chapter, we'll learn about Justin's story, how one simple action after his father died changed the entire direction of his life.

First, let's peek at what we've learned in this chapter...

GOOD MOURNING INSIGHTS

- Choose to find happiness again. Your lost loved one wouldn't want it any other way.
- You can tap into the types of happy things you shared with your loved one, or you can play the glad game to find something new.
- Sometimes the "surface level" things that make us happy can lead to deeply rooted ways to help us heal.
- *Bonus Happiness Tip*: Grab your dog, or any dog, and start a staring contest with them. According to research published in *Science Magazine*,[19] your happiness can sky-rocket 300 percent just by looking deep into your dog's eyes. Don't worry, you won't be the only one benefiting from this passionate encounter. Your dog's happiness will increase by 130 percent, too! Go find a dog right now—I "stare" you...

CHAPTER 8

ACTION—JUSTIN TIME FOR DINNER

"Action is the antidote to despair."

—JOAN BAEZ

I'd rather eat crickets than Mom's chicken divan.

When she plopped a generous helping of the nightmare casserole on my plate, I wouldn't touch it. The thought of placing my least favorite vegetable on God's green earth—mushy broccoli—into my mouth made me tearful. Literally tearful. Mom had no sympathy. Not one iota. No matter how long it took, I had to sit at the kitchen table until every last bite of the green goo was gone.

Little did she know, I always came to the table with reinforcements hidden under my shirt—lots and lots of napkins. Like magic, the concoction atop my plate would disappear, bite by bite, into the rescue napkins.

"Wow, Jen, great job! You finished everything like a good girl," she congratulated me, with just a small hint of sarcasm. I knew she was on to me and my napkin trick. Before I was excused to the safety of the basement, she lifted my plate to see a ring of crumpled napkins, each filled with its own gently chewed chicken and broccoli divan inside.

"Jenny, there are starving people in this world. You don't know how lucky you are to have this food." I wasn't fazed. Then she hit me where it hurt most. She revoked my dessert privileges—a devastating punishment. "Absolutely NO chocolate ice cream tonight. Do you hear me? Now, go about your business." After receiving that dreadful verdict, I slinked to my downstairs hideaway.

I returned to the scene of my non-eating crime about an hour later and began circling Mom as she put the last of the dishes away. She was no fool. I was up there for one thing and one thing only.

"Mom, can I pleeease have some ice cream?" I begged.

She couldn't help herself. She caved, but it came at a price. "Oh, go ahead. But you're getting a big bag of carrots in your lunch tomorrow, and you better not throw them away! Eat them for your health."

As I grew up, I learned to appreciate Mom and the good food she provided. In this particular incident, I was learning a good, old-fashioned life lesson, one that showed up later in my childhood. It was as if God Himself wanted me to know how incredibly lucky I was to have the life, the mother, and the food I had been given. I just didn't think that lesson would involve the dreaded chicken divan casserole again.

But it did.

There I was sitting in the musty, cold cafeteria of St. Mary's with fifty classmates. We were only thinking of our one common goal: to make Confirmation the next fall. The director stood before us with a few housekeeping announcements before we went to our classrooms. She ended with a rather large request. "Okay, before we split off into groups, we need one of you to fill a very important role. We need someone to lead a new casserole program at the soup kitchen in downtown Baltimore."

I scanned the room. Not a soul raised their hand. Enjoying the security of blending in, I hadn't either. Then suddenly, my arm shot up as if God Himself had raised it for me. "I'll do it," I said under my breath.

"That's great, Jenny. See me after class," she replied.

The night came and went faster than ever. At the end of the evening, I edged my way to the door, hoping my very public casserole commitment had been forgotten.

But no. I heard my name shouted out, echoing off the walls. "Jenny! In here. I'll show you what needs to be done for next Monday."

"Okay..." I stammered.

"Now, here are the aluminum pans. You'll need to place these in the vestibule before Sunday. Father will announce our need for fifty casseroles."

I didn't have words. I stared at the fifty pans like a deer in headlights.

"Oh, look, your mom's here. Have a good night. And thank you for stepping up," she said, patting me gently on my shoulder.

What have I done? How am I going to make this happen? I can't drive. I don't know how to make a casserole.

When Mom pulled up, my stomach went sour, as if I'd just taken a bite of chicken divan. I trembled, afraid to break the news, as I walked to the car.

"Hey, Jen, how was class tonight?" she inquired.

"Well, Mom, I kinda told the director I'd help lead a casserole program for the church."

An eternity passed as I waited for her to respond. All she said was, "Oh, that's great, Jen. I'm so proud of you."

"You are?" I replied.

"Absolutely. You saw a need and took action," she said proudly.

"Well, I'm glad you think so. Because I'm responsible for driving these casseroles down to Baltimore the first Monday of every month."

"Ohhh, really? How are you going to do that?" she asked.

"I was hoping you'd help me," I said tentatively.

"Okay, Jen, we'll figure it out. Don't worry," she reassured me.

When the first Monday rolled around, Mom let me take the morning off school so we could deliver the casseroles together. My heart was full of pride as we arrived at the soup kitchen on Bond Street. It was the perfect street name. Mom and I shared a special bond in this experience. It also represented who my mother was. Whenever she made a promise, she kept it. Her word was her bond.

The volunteers had us park inside the gate to make unloading the trunk full of casseroles easier. As they placed the pans in an old shopping cart, Mom and I grabbed the non-food donations from the back seat and took them to the office. When we said our goodbyes, Mom touched my arm and gave it a little hug, which was her way of saying, "I'm proud of you." On our way back, I couldn't stop talking about how great it felt to help people in need. Mom just listened.

After three months of casserole delivery, my enthusiasm waned. Mom stopped asking me to go and simply took the program on full time. I had committed to it, yet she took it on willingly. For the next seventeen years, like clockwork, Mom loaded and dropped off a trunk-load of casseroles every month. That's 10,200 casseroles, with one casserole feeding twelve people. That means my mom helped feed over 122,000 people in that period.

This selfless act came full circle after she was diagnosed. Her dear friend Barb started a casserole program for our family. Though Mom didn't have much appetite to enjoy the fruits of her friends' labor, she was able to appreciate their love.

Our family did enjoy many of the casseroles as we cared for Mom in her final days. While they warmed in the oven, I would close my eyes and imagine Mom standing in front of the kitchen sink, laughing at my failed attempts to hide chicken divan under my plate. I would give anything to go back in time to that chicken divan day, yet I still connect with her when I sit down at our family table.

Justin Thongsavanh found he could connect, through dinners, with an important person he lost, too.

His father, Tom, died when Justin was twelve. Just a boy, he never felt more alone in his life. "I was becoming a moody teenager," he explained, "and that made this very adult emotion of losing my father even harder to deal with." He found a ray of hope early in his *good mourning* journey through Pauline, who would soon become his best friend. She had lost her father at a young age, too. She was a breath of fresh air for Justin and made him realize how important it was to find someone who could understand his pain.

He sought and found solace by surrounding himself with good people like Pauline. He found empathy and understanding in people who had been through something similar. "That's what helped me get through my hardest days without my father. Talking and connecting with people who all had experienced loss. They were willing to sit and chat about it, even if they barely knew me," he said.

After learning this valuable lesson, he dedicated his life to helping others connect and heal after loss. Once he graduated from California State University, he went to Comfort Zone Camp, a camping experience that provides positive healing for children who have lost one or both parents. He volunteered at first and then became a full-time counselor for several years.

When he saw all the children connecting, he felt like he had hit the reset button on his grief, and feelings of loss returned and flooded him. He missed the comfort of having kindred spirits to connect with, like Pauline. That's when he found an ad for something called The Dinner Party. This organization helps people in their twenties and thirties connect with others who have suffered a significant loss in their lives. They gather for a potluck dinner (and maybe a casserole) while connecting with each other in an environment of mutual understanding.

His first Dinner Party was exactly what he needed. "I just started to share my story," he said. The rest was history. From there, they all built friendships with relatedness that led them to have necessary, if not always easy, conversations. "We quickly got candid and talked about things like getting married without your parent who has died but whose memory is still very much a part of your life."

The experience of talking about the death of someone we love can be like Justin's first Dinner Party. In the beginning, it's tough to bring up something so personal in front of strangers. When we open up and let our feelings out in a safe space, we make room for healing to take place. That's how Justin got back on his *good mourning* path. He became a regular at Dinner Party get-togethers and then decided to join the small, robust staff of this phenomenal organization as operations and partnerships manager.

In his position, he has the distinct pleasure of finding the best programs and organizations available and connecting people with them—a role he was born for. Through these partnerships, people have the chance to connect over loss while having fun, too. One of his most recent coups was partnering with Outward Bound, an experience-based outdoor leadership training organization for young adults.

His *good mourning* journey all started with one simple action, going to his first Dinner Party. There he found he could make a difference not only in his life but in the lives of thousands. To date, he has helped over 10,000 people talk about their grief at over 275 dinner tables led by 313 volunteer hosts in nearly 100 cities and towns in more than six countries.[20]

Justin's work allows him to continue to heal and mourn his dad's loss. "I love the work I do in the sense that I know my dad would be really proud of me for being able to give back to a community of people who don't really have a lot

---

20   "About Us." Dinnerparty.com, www.thedinnerparty.org/about

of resources. Being a part of The Dinner Party staff lets me honor my dad."

As long as Justin is in action helping others in grief, his father lives on. My mother never stopped helping and loving others. I strive to follow in her footsteps in creating my *good mourning* journey, where she lives on. My aim is to soothe the hurting souls of those in mourning.

One thing I did was create a one-of-a-kind event in downtown Baltimore not far from the soup kitchen Mom and I went to all those years ago. My dear motherless friend, Jackie Morrison, was the co-host. We had a full line-up of gigs that helped our fellow mourners smile again. Guests mingled to the tinkling of show tunes on the piano and sported custom balloon hats. Fifty people and a handful of passers-by were there. None of these lives would have been impacted had we not first taken action.

If you feel called to do something, *anything*, on your *good mourning* journey, just follow your instincts. You never know where they'll lead. Justin was able to use his loss as the start of a rewarding career. I've been able to transform my grief over my mother's death into helping people get the most out of their *good mourning* journeys. No matter how big, small, or even zany your idea is, you never know who you may help. It could even be you.

In the next chapter, we'll learn how Anisha began to heal on her *good mourning* journey by celebrating a victory.

First, let's take a look at what we've gathered from this chapter...

GOOD MOURNING INSIGHTS
- Taking action, even reluctant action at first, can be a life-changer. Your true destiny could be revealed.
- The impact of your actions can be massive.
- Serving someone else can pull you out of your grief and make you a *good mourning* person.

CHAPTER 9

VICTORY—ANISHA'S FOR LETTER OR WORSE

—

"Victory at all costs, victory in spite of all terror, victory however long and hard the road may be; for without victory, there is no survival."

—WINSTON CHURCHILL

For me, doing dumb things came in successive waves.

Like insisting the long, wooden handle would NOT nail me in the forehead the moment I stomped on the rake's sharp teeth. Turns out, it does, and I have the permanent mark to prove it.

But this stunt topped them all. I was caught cheating on my English exam.

On my way home from school that day, I was eager to soothe my guilty conscience. So I did something impulsive and stupid. I picked up a hitchhiker. The woman I stopped for didn't exactly have her thumb up. I happened to notice a large, bright-colored image in my periphery as I passed a stretch of trees. I looked again and saw a woman lying on the side of the road next to her bicycle. Alarmed, I pulled into the closest driveway and slowly approached to see if she was all right.

"Umm, ma'am, is everything okay?" I said softly while leaning toward my car for a quick getaway.

She lay completely still in the grass, only moving her eyes to blink before replying, "Yeaaahhh, I just got really tired coming up that big hill."

I decided to be helpful to redeem myself. I picked up her bike, shoved it in my tiny trunk, and drove her to her house. As I left her driveway, I wanted to go anywhere but home. I was beyond ashamed and knew Mom would be so disappointed in me, now for two things instead of one—cheating and picking up a hitchhiker. When I neared the hill before our home, I prayed she wouldn't be there. But her car was in its usual spot. It was a gorgeous day, so I found her mowing the lawn. Seeing me, she turned the tractor off and walked over.

"How was your day, Jen?" she said with a smile.

"I picked up a hitchhiker!" I blurted out without even thinking.

Since I couldn't unsay it, I had hoped this good deed would somehow lessen the blow of the cheating incident.

"Uh, what?" she exclaimed.

"Yes, I saw this woman lying at the side of the road, so I took her home."

"Jenny, that is so dangerous. It could have been a trap! Don't ever do that again. You hear me?"

"Okay, Mom, I won't," I mumbled. Then I added, "I have something else to tell you."

As I worked myself up to unveil the next portion of my bad news, I looked down to the ground to avoid seeing her reaction. A puddle of tears started forming on the blacktop before I got out what I needed to tell her. "I was caught cheating on my English test today." I stopped, took a breath and continued, "And you and I have to go back to school tonight for a meeting with my teacher and the board of the National Honor Society."

Mom was an empathetic person. When I looked up, I saw her crying, too. She took a tissue out of her pocket to wipe, first, my tears and then hers. All she could say was, "Okay, Jen. We'll go."

"I have to go inside now and prepare something to say to my teacher and the board," I said.

She nodded and got back on the mower to finish the lawn.

It felt like I was staring at the blank computer screen for days. I didn't know what to say. I was guilty, and that was it. Then suddenly, I heard Mom approach. I looked over to see her carrying a book. As she got closer, I realized it was the Holy Bible.

She grabbed the red ribbon she was using for a marker and flipped to Psalms 119:105 and read, "*Your word is a lamp to my feet and a light to my path.* When we're struggling with something we've done wrong, all you have to do is have faith and trust in God that he's with you to help you through it," she said. Next, she placed the Bible in front of me. "You should include this in your talk tonight."

I did.

My teacher and the members of the National Honor Society (NHS) board were so moved by my letter and palpable remorse, they allowed me to remain in the NHS. I declined their offer, even though I appreciated it. Knowing what I had done, I could not morally continue to associate myself with the organization. They didn't take me off the roster, but I told myself that night I wouldn't go to future events or get-togethers.

On our way home, Mom grabbed my hand and said, "I was so proud of you tonight, Jen. You did the right thing." I didn't answer, but I knew deep down that I had. It was one of my very first victories—doing what I knew was the right thing in the face of turmoil. I had Mom right by my side as I read that letter, supporting me the whole time.

I was reminded of this victory when I first met Anisha Weimer. Hers was a victory in the face of profound grief.

The morning her father Bruce died she remembers looking for him everywhere. "Dad, come on, it's time for church," she yelled, at the same time wondering, *Where is he?*

If your dad was the "Our Whole Lives" aka "sex ed" teacher at your church, you'd normally be hiding under the covers to avoid the intense awkwardness. Not Anisha. She loved having her very respectful, open, and real dad be the one to tell her and her friends about contraception. She could talk to her dad about anything. That's just the type of bond they shared.

When she still couldn't find him, she called her mom who was at the gym. She told Anisha to go downstairs to the basement. "He may be exercising on the cross-country machine," she told her. There was her loving father lying on the floor. An avid runner, Bruce had a rare heart condition that cut his life short. Nothing, not even CPR, could bring him back. He was gone.

Though Anisha and her family were devastated by the sudden and tragic loss, they found comfort in knowing Bruce died doing something he loved—running. And, equally comforting was knowing he breathed his last breath in the beloved home he had helped build, paint, and remodel himself.

Unfortunately for Anisha, her mother, and sister, they couldn't afford their dream home with him gone. Their hearts were filled with sorrow as they bid farewell to the house that held memories of their life as a family. He had given his all to create the home of their dreams. Soon after it went on the market, they found a buyer—a family with young kids.

While Anisha could have easily been sad about having to leave her home, she wasn't. She decided to take the high road and wrote the new homeowners a letter. On settlement day, she handed it over to them. It read…

Dear New Owners of the Weimer Family Home,

You're going to have a great time in this house. As you know, my father passed away, and that's the reason we had to give it up. We can no longer afford to stay here.

While that makes me sad, I'm really happy we're passing it on to you. And I hope you make lots of memories here. I do hope you respect the work my dad did on the house. He worked very hard to keep it nice for us.

We understand if you want to make changes. It is your house, after all. But know this house is part of my dad, so please cherish it.

With Love,

Anisha Weimer

As the young family stood on the back patio reading her letter, they couldn't hold the tears back. They looked over to Anisha, her sister, and mother as they said, "Oh, my gosh.

Wow, thank you so much." Now, if that letter wasn't a victory, I don't know what is. Anisha's courage shone through and she knew her dad was watching over her the whole time. Most of all, it's given her the strength to continue to have a *good mourning* to this day.

I say this a lot, and it bears repeating. We can't change our situations, but we can change how we approach each new day, each new challenge, each new victory. We have a choice to embrace them, for "letter" or for worse.

You may be wondering what kind of victory you could have. You might go through your loved one's belongings and donate them to charity. Or you might go to your loved one's favorite restaurant. These victories may hurt at first, but they help us grow. They give us the strength to face the challenges that pop up on our path.

My moment of victory came in randomly encountering a T-Rex named Sue in The Field Museum of Chicago.

In the first months of my journey, I couldn't bear to hear my mom's name, Sue. I even had to remove Johnny Cash's "A Boy Named Sue" from my phone because it triggered sadness. What makes triggers like these so confronting is that they happen when you least expect them. They can be a familiar smell, memory, song, food, or anything that reminds us of the person we lost.

What I came to discover was if I could just get past the initial sting of seeing or hearing my mom's name, it could actually make me happy. Sue the T-Rex was that for me. In 1990, Sue

Hendrickson discovered Sue, the most complete and biggest T-Rex ever found to that date. She named it Sue, after herself. And accidentally, she named it after my mom.

Seeing the signs all around the museum asking if we had seen Sue, along with all the "Sue"venirs in the gift shop, soothed my trigger and had me embrace this almost comical use of my mother's name. I bought blankets, books, mugs—you name it—with the picture of a T-Rex named "Sue" on it.

I think I have single-handedly funded Sue Hendrickson's next dinosaur expedition. Every item was a happy reminder that I embraced Sue with open arms, even if Sue's arms were too tiny to hug me in return. The name "Sue" was now associated not just with my mother but with a dinosaur. It was a small victory on my *good mourning* journey.

A museum wasn't where I thought I would have a victory over grief. What's so exciting about this journey is that big and small victories can happen all the time, for you, too.

I can't wait for you to meet Anthony in the next chapter. When his mom died, he invested in a whole business dedicated to spreading love in the world.

First, let's review everything we've learned in this chapter…

GOOD MOURNING INSIGHTS
- Triggers can happen in the most unexpected places. Embracing them can lead us to hold them as wonderful memories instead of painful grief.

- The more we embrace triggers, the sooner we begin to heal.
- Victories can come in all shapes and sizes, even letters and dinosaurs.
- Doing the right thing in the face of turmoil can be a victory you will never forget.

CHAPTER 10

EXPRESSION— ANTHONY'S GOOD NEWS

———

"Beauty without expression is boring."

—RALPH WALDO EMERSON

"They can use their hooves as cups."

I shot my arm in the air as if I had just discovered gravity and blurted this "hoof" discovery out with zero inhibition. We were brainstorming ways Native Americans could use parts of a bison in my fifth-grade classroom. The obvious using the hide as a blanket was taken. After scanning the picture of the big, brown beast, that gem of an answer appeared in my wacky ten-year-old brain.

Expressing myself was not something I had trouble with— clearly. It did, however, get me into a lot of trouble later that day when we split into dialogue groups. Our teacher had us open our books, and there it was. A sketch of a chief on the first page, buck naked, except for a tiny patch of skillful shading.

My classmates' mouths were agape, but I wasn't embarrassed. I looked and snapped back with, "What? You can't see his privates." That rather forward comment was all it took for my teacher to send me to the hallway. My innocent expression of the obvious was out-of-the-box for what was acceptable in the social norms of the school. I slunk down in my chair and fiddled with my half-chewed thumbnails while I watched the class through the side window.

Five minutes later, I heard the familiar clinking of my mom's keys. Then I remembered she was coming to school that day to help out. "Jenny, what are you doing out in the hall?" she demanded.

I looked down at my nubby thumbs. "Umm, I got in trouble," I replied, ashamed.

Seeing Mom talking with me, my teacher came out and explained what had happened.

Mom used every muscle in her face to hold back her laughter, but a loud chuckle escaped her freshly painted lips anyway. I breathed a sigh of relief. I was in the clear. My teacher wasn't amused. He told both of us my incendiary comment was bound to cause a stir among the other parents, forcing him to explain the verbal slip-up I had made.

Mom composed herself and said with remorse, "I'm so sorry. I will be sure to talk to Jenny later."

She never did.

I tell you this little story because it's an example of when I operated outside the safe zone. When we're in mourning, we're programmed to operate in a familiar zone that puts us and our feelings into a neatly wrapped box. Our expression of grief has to be carefully curated to match society's expectations. Often, these expressions of grief need to be paired with undertones of deep sorrow to be acceptable.

In her journal article, "Stifled Grief: How the West Has It Wrong,"[21] Michelle Steinke-Baumgard spoke of this box. She believes most mourners will end up in one if they're not careful.

She explains, *"Western society has created a neat little 'grief box' where we place the grieving and wait for them to emerge, fixed and whole again. The grief box is small and compact, and it comes full of expectations that range from time frames to physical appearance. Everyone who has been pushed into the grief box understands its confining limitations, but all of our collective voices together can't seem to change the intense indignation of a society too emotionally stifled to speak the truth. It's become easier to hide our emotional depth than to reveal our vulnerability and risk harsh judgment. When asked*

---

21 Steinke-Baumgard, Michelle. "Stifled Grief: How the West Has It Wrong." Huffpost.com, www.huffpost.com/entry/stifled-grief-how-the-wes_b_10243026

if we are all right, it's simpler to say yes and fake a smile than to be honest and show genuine human emotion."

I couldn't agree more.

It would have been way easier for me to not write this book, but I felt too strongly about the power of having a *good mourning* not to have written it. I'd rather *"reveal my vulnerability and risk harsh judgment,"* as the author put it, than keep my grieving mouth shut. Each time I express myself around my mom's death, intense healing abounds.

During the writing process, I have learned a valuable lesson. This book and its message won't please everyone. Its contents may resonate with some and completely escape others. Either way, I can sleep soundly knowing I stepped outside the grief box and expressed my truth.

I was blessed to find another out-of-the-box griever who has enriched my *good mourning* journey greatly.

Anthony Samadani is a highly successful entrepreneur. I found an episode featuring his story on the podcast *Pray,* entitled *"Tragedies Determine How We Live."* In it, he gives an account of the loss of his mother Sherry. It was Valentine's Day, 2009. He described his mother's passing on the evening she died, *"My dad walks into the room and sees her praying. She gets up from prayer and asks him for a glass of water. She sits next to him and says, 'I love you and you've been a great husband, but I have to go now.' She then faints, falls directly on her prayer rug, and dies."*

I called to interview him about his mother's poetic yet miraculous death. He told me that once word got out about Sherry's passing, religious leaders from the Muslim community inquired, "How was it your mother was honored to die like that?"

Anthony's response was as simple as his mother's beauty. "She believed in God. She didn't do anything extraordinary regarding religious stuff. She just tried to do as much good as she could every day for other people and herself."

I found comfort in his words because my mom was like his. She, too, just tried to do as much good as she could every day. Anthony had the courage to tell his mother's story, and I found deep healing for my own loss in his message. What he said next was a huge blessing to me on my *good mourning* journey. "I never looked at my mother's death as a tragedy. I just shifted my focus from this life to the next. I now focus on all the good she did, and I know I'll see her again."

With this, he discovered something very fundamentally human. Everyone has the same purpose: to do good for others and themselves every single day. What a freeing statement. It is not only practical, but it gives each of us something to strive for. To put this revelation into action, he decided to become co-owner of the Good News Network (GNN).

GNN is a website with more than twenty thousand positive news stories from all over the globe. Millions of followers use it to drown out negativity in the media. GNN is so popular, it's ranked #1 on Google[22] for "good news." Along with founder Geri Weis-Corbley, Anthony offers heartwarming stories to inspire people to leave behind a legacy to "do good for yourself and others every single day."

Some inspiring headlines include:

- *American Brothers Successfully Save Irish Girl Swept out to Sea in Serendipitous Twist of Fate*[23]
- *VHS Tape of Baby Taking First Steps Is Finally Returned to Family After Man Found It Inside a Used TV*[24]
- *Rather Than Slip into Depression, Man Quits Job, Sells Possessions, and Travels the World with a Ferret*[25]

What's not to love about these? If you want to read these articles and thousands more, they're available on goodnewsnetwork.org. They'll not only make you feel good, but they could also inspire you to speak your truth about loss in a way that helps you have a *good mourning.*

---

22 "About Us." Goodnewsnetwork.com, www.goodnewsnetwork.org

23 Corbley, McKinley. "American Brothers Successfully Save Irish Girl Who Was Swept out to Sea in Serendipitous Twist of Fate." Goodnewsnetwork. org, www.goodnewsnetwork.org/brothers-save-irish-girl-at-sea-in-serendipitous-twist-of-fate/

24 Corbley, McKinley. "VHS Tape of Baby Taking First Steps Is Finally Returned to Family After Man Found It Inside a Used TV." Goodnewsnetwork.org, www.goodnewsnetwork.org/vhs-tape-of-baby-taking-first-steps-returned-to-family/

25 "Rather Than Slip into Depression, Man Quits Job, Sells Possessions, and Travels the World with a Ferret." Goodnewsnetwork.org, www.goodnewsnetwork.org/airman-quits-job-and-travels-world-with-ferret/

Anthony believes that when we do good for ourselves first by speaking our truth and attending to our needs, we're then able to go out in the world to help and give to others. He even created a simple equation for us to see the true value of our efforts. It is self-worth.

Self (more) *giving to yourself* + Self (less) *giving to others* = self-worth

If you begin to follow Anthony's lead, you might soon be spouting off whatever comes to your mind, just like I did in my fifth-grade classroom. You might even find yourself writing a book about your own *good mourning* journey or start a good news website like Anthony's. You might even come up with something that hasn't even been invented yet like "Ferret Finder for Grievers." Who knows?

The beauty of this *good mourning* journey is that you never know what could transpire in the days to come. I've learned you must first express your truth, whatever it is. Then share your feelings, your emotions, and your story with others. I can attest that it's one of the most healing, transformative experiences you'll ever have. Your self-worth will follow, which is key. With it, you can change the world.

The best complement to finding your own ways to express your grief and mourn with joy is to find your own alliances. In the next chapter, you'll meet a dear friend of mine, Bobby Marsee, who found his while on a bike.

First, let's look at the important lessons we learned...

GOOD MOURNING INSIGHTS

- Whatever your experience is about loss, speak it. You don't know who it might help.
- We all have the same purpose: do good for yourself and others every day.
- Self (more) *giving to yourself* + Self (less) *giving to others* = self-worth
- When you operate outside the "safe zone," people may not agree. However, it's where you can leave a legacy of contribution to others.
- Don't let others put you in a grief box and tell you how to grieve. It's yours; express it your way.

CHAPTER 11

ALLIANCE—BOBBY'S STROKE OF LUCK

---

*"Alone, we can do so little; together,
we can do so much."*

—HELEN KELLER

As a kid, I was hypnotized by a big, gray anthropomorphic rat.

He wore a red and yellow top hat and made the best pepperoni pizza around.

The moment he turned his robotic head in my direction to wink, I blushed. He had eleven-year-old me wrapped around his furry little claw. When I heard the faint speaker discreetly tucked behind his incisors say, "Welcome to Chuck E. Cheese! I'm so glad you're here," I knew I was home.

My sisters and I begged Mom to take us there every chance we got. We shoved melodramatic letters under her door, promising to wash her dirty socks for all eternity. We swarmed outside her bedroom like hornets waiting for the verdict. All of a sudden, she appeared with a cheesy grin on her face. Cheesier than Chuck E.'s. We weren't sure if her smile was the result of our outlandish empty promises, or if Chuck E. had put his lovestruck spell on her, too. Nevertheless, we were ecstatic.

That was until she told us we had to take a necessary detour to St. Joseph's hospital to get her paycheck. I pouted the whole way there. At that age, I didn't realize how incredibly selfless her gesture of collecting her wages so we could go play and eat was. When we arrived in the parking lot, my pouting turned to abject fear when I was faced with this earth-shattering ultimatum…

"Jenny, your sisters are asleep. Can you please go up to the ICU and get my check for me?"

I trembled in the backseat, debating if I should heed her frightening request or not. If I succeeded, the rewards would be immense. There would be a cardboard cup filled to the brim with tokens and a slice of pizza with my name on it. If I was a coward and forced her to park and wake my sisters up, I feared she might change her mind and take us home. I wasn't going to tempt fate that morning, so I got out of the car.

It was the first time I had ever walked into a busy hospital or ridden in an elevator all by myself. I wanted to turn back, but Chuck E. Cheese beckoned. I bit the bullet and did what we came here to do. I was on a mission to get the check.

The elevator stopped at the ICU floor, and I approached the first friendly face I saw. "Ummm, excuse me…" Before I got a chance to even finish, the woman burst in asking, "Are you Sue Hale's daughter?"

"Yeahhhh," I replied bashfully.

"Awww! You look just like her. I'm your mom's friend. Which one are you?"

"I'm Jenny."

"Oh, you're the middle child. Right?" she asked.

"Yes, I am."

"Girls, come over here! This is Sue's daughter."

Hordes of nurses came to greet me. They gushed over me. Some of them hugged me. I was embarrassed and even a bit taken aback by this red-carpet treatment. It made me wonder, *Why are they being so nice to me?* As I scanned the circle of doting women, I saw that some had white scrubs, and others wore dark-blue cardigans. Black and silver stethoscopes adorned a few women's necks. They *all* had one thing in common: big, warm smiles. I realized the reason they were being so nice to me was because of my mom.

I was so caught up in the commotion, I almost forgot the check. "Do you have my mom's check?" I asked her friend at the front desk.

"Oh, sure, sweetie, let me go get it. What are you girls up today? Something fun?"

"Chuck E. Cheese," I said.

"Aw, that Sue. Always doing something nice for her girls." She handed me the check and escorted me back to the car to see Mom.

I am so glad I didn't chicken out that day. Not just because we got to go to Chuck E. Cheese but more because I got a glimpse into Mom's world. It was a world full of love, companionship, and kindness. It made an impression on me even at that young age. As an adult, the memory of that day made me appreciate the woman she was all the more. It also made me realize that her co-workers were very important to her.

Based on what I witnessed that day, Mom was part of something stronger than family. It was an alliance of selfless, compassionate people. They had dedicated their lives to helping and loving their patients and, most of all, to loving each other. They were family. This alliance grew and grew as Mom changed the course of her career, next becoming a community health nurse and then a school nurse at various local middle schools. Being the selfless, loving woman she was, she simply attracted more and more of these incredible people who made up her tribe.

This alliance came out in full force when she got sick. The moment these amazing women heard of Mom's terminal diagnosis, they dropped everything to call, text, email, or visit her right away. They made casseroles. They hand-knitted her blankets and scarves. These women gave Mom the strength to keep moving forward when she barely had the strength to sit up. Though she would've done the same for them, Mom was floored by their generosity and thoughtfulness. She reciprocated as long as she could with thank you texts, emails, and handwritten notes.

When she died, these women all attended her viewing and funeral. They created a walking team and raised money to fight cancer. They acknowledged the woman she was at her life celebration event. They continued to honor her by supporting me with this book venture. If it weren't for the love so many of these women had for Mom, you wouldn't be holding this book in your hands right now. That's how powerful this alliance is. It's now eternal.

Sometimes in life, we meet people that we become instant friends with. Like Bert and Ernie. Or me and Chuck E. Or we simply attract people who are meant to be in our circle, like Mom and her nursing friends. These friends quickly become our lifeline when an unspoken alliance is formed. The same rings true for a very special buddy of mine, Bobby Marsee, and his dear friend, Barbara. They met at a local art show in Barbara's hometown of Clinton, Oklahoma. It was a lucky encounter that would enrich his life forever.

After setting up their individual booths with their paintings, they waited for the crowds to appear. Barbara noticed the skillfulness of Bobby's work and walked over to introduce herself and ask about it. Her next question would change the course of his life. "Do you give lessons? I took up painting after my husband died, and I have always wanted to become a better artist."

He had to think on his feet because he didn't give lessons and didn't have any plans to. Not wanting to disappoint, he simply answered, "Yes." She was so elated with his answer, she promised to bring a bevy of friends along to make it worth his while. Barbara was a woman of her word. A week later, she and three friends met Bobby at her church with fresh brushes in hand and hope in their eyes. The painting group became so popular, three quickly became eight, requiring them to find a bigger space. That's when Bobby offered up his picture framing studio just a short drive away.

Barbara religiously attended Bobby's classes. She had one goal: to paint a portrait of her late husband. When Bobby learned of her plan, he worked tirelessly to help her make it happen. She finally succeeded and lauded it as her favorite painting. She continued her lessons well after this achievement and ultimately formed a special bond with Bobby. She was more than just a loyal patron. She was a surrogate grandmother, buying him little *"I had to get this for you"* gifts and ending many texts with *I love you.*

When Barbara got sick with lymphoma, Bobby was heartbroken. He wanted to do more for her than just offer prayer. One day after her lesson, he said, "So there's this organization called Team in Training. It's a cycling program organized to raise money for blood cancer research. Would you feel weird if I raised money in your name?"

Her response was indicative of the amazing human being she was. "Of course not. I will help you."

Barbara was a beloved person around town. Whenever someone said her name, smiles appeared on people's faces. Everyone loved her. Those smiles quickly turned into lots of dollars. By race day, she and Bobby had raised nearly twelve thousand dollars, even though Barbara was going through chemo and was very weak throughout their campaign. Before the race, she asked Bobby to drop by her house. She greeted him with a huge hug and handed him a small bag. The item inside became one of his most cherished possessions. It was a T-shirt that read *Friends Ride Together*.

Her encouragement didn't stop there. While Bobby was riding, she left him messages on his Facebook page like, *I'll be pushing you up the hill*. Her efforts helped make Bobby's first race a smashing success. When he came home, he and Barbara started making plans for the following year. Barbara's lymphoma was in remission, and she felt great. However, Bobby needed hip surgery, forcing him to forego his second race. The moment he recovered, he and Barbara were back at it. Instead of going door to door for donations, they hosted a silent auction and benefit in town. Every single one of the ten tables were gobbled up in an instant, and they achieved double their fundraising goal. Barbara was beyond thrilled.

Then she found out the cancer had come back. She started chemo again and felt well enough to continue going to painting class. Then, just like that, she stopped. Bobby visited with her and discovered she just couldn't handle any more painting, or anymore anything. The cancer took Barbara a few months later.

Shattered by his loss, Bobby got back on his bike and started raising money again. One day, as Bobby was on the Team in Training support page, a fellow Okie named Lauri contacted him. She introduced herself and let him know she was planning to ride in the next race, too. Like Bobby, Lauri's a genuine, friendly person, so she invited him to ride with her on weekends since she lived just a few towns over. Training took several hours each time, so they got acquainted fast and soon became great friends. Then, on race day at the sign-in table, they met yet another Okie named Jerry. Bobby, Lauri, and Jerry stayed with and pushed each other the whole way, ultimately forming their "Three Amigos" alliance.

That's how Bobby and I became friends, too. We met at my first Team in Training century (one hundred miles) ride, and I was doing it in memory of Mom. We talked and then instantly bonded the moment we both noticed and laughed about one cycling enthusiast's overinflated calf muscles at the starting line. I knew I had found a kindred spirit. I was nervous because this was my first century ride, and his sense of humor put me at ease.

Bobby covered basic hand and verbal communication signals with me just minutes before the race began. "The most important signal you need to know is 'Car up' because it means a car is coming toward us," he said. I nodded and off we went. We had several miles ahead of us, so we got to talking. He told me all about his painting career and studio and his life in Oklahoma with his lovely wife Angela and two rescue dogs. He also told me about Barbara, which gave me the opening to tell him about Mom.

Before the mood got too serious, he screamed, "Squirrel up!" It wasn't a real bike cue at all. As soon as I saw the hungry little varmint munching on an acorn, I laughed so hard I almost fell off my bike. Of course, screaming "squirrel up" became a thing for the next one hundred miles, squirrel or no squirrel in sight.

I feel blessed to call Bobby my friend. Countless Team in Training riders also became friends. If it hadn't been for his dedication to Barbara and his Team in Training riding crew, he could never have imagined planning a cycling event with his friends, Jerry and Lauri, to help raise money for people affected by cancer in Oklahoma. When I heard of his plans, I wasn't surprised. Not just because it is reflective of who Bobby is but more so because of the power that alliances can have in our lives.

When we're in mourning, we may want to isolate ourselves. We want to retreat and be alone as a way to avoid any further hurt. From my experience, that does more damage than good. That's why I encourage you to find your tribe, your alliance with intention. Find a community on steroids, if you will, that pushes you to create a better version of yourself as you move along in your own *good mourning* journey.

In the next chapter, you'll meet a wonderful man named Dan whose generosity helped him become a better version of himself after his wife died.

Let's take a peek at what we've discovered in this chapter...

GOOD MOURNING INSIGHTS

- Don't isolate yourself from the world.
- Stop and take a look at people you're close to in your life. Who are the people they are in alliance with? Notice the love.
- Find your tribe, your people, your alliance to become a better version of yourself.
- When you find your alliance, you can go on to create bigger and better things in this world.
- If you want to go to Chuck E. Cheese, promise to wash your mom's socks for all eternity.

CHAPTER 12

GENEROSITY—DAN'S BETTER HALF

———

"No one has ever become poor by giving."

—ANNE FRANK

I hated the last day of school with a capital "H."

Before thoughts of summer fun and running through the sprinkler, eating cherry push-pops, and catching lightning bugs could even emerge, I had to do one thing that I dreaded more than anything else. Mom gave me the very embarrassing job of distributing gifts to every single one of the teachers, custodians, secretaries, and cafeteria staff at my elementary school.

These weren't just any generic, last-minute gifts you'd pick up from the pharmacy or grocery store. They were items custom-picked to match the recipients' interests, hobbies, and likes. Mom not only had a tremendous heart but a keen ear. She was always on alert for tidbits about people's lives, ones she could use for ideas for future gifts.

Those ideas were wrapped, tagged, and stuffed into two large green shopping bags waiting for me at the front door. I waddled down to the bus stop with one monstrosity in each hand. When I got to school, I placed them in the closet, secretly hoping they'd be mistaken for trash by the custodian. Much to my dismay, they were there still waiting for me when the final bell of the school year rang. While the other kids ran out the doors to start their summer vacations, I made my way around the school, slowly chipping away at the massive sacks full of goodies.

I made pit stops with every single person employed by the school. Thinking I was finally a free bird, I was not quite done. I felt something jiggle around in the bottom of my bag. When I saw what it was and who it was for, I made my way to the vacant gymnasium and breathed a sigh of relief. I thought my gym teacher had already left for summer. Then I heard a basketball hit the ground in the storage closet and walked toward it. Not wanting to startle him, I cleared my throat so he would turn around. "Ummm, my mom wanted you to have this."

I reached into the bag and handed him a box of Good and Plenty candy, my mother's favorite treat, with a big blue bow on top. I don't have a clue whether he liked them or not, or if Mom had somehow found out they were his favorite, too. All I knew was that 99-cent box of candy put a million-dollar smile on his face. "Wow, Jenny, thank you very much. Tell your mom thanks, too."

I then did what any ten-year-old would do. I hightailed it out of there faster than you could say "candy." My deeds were done, and summer could begin.

I love thinking of this story now, especially the irony of giving a box of sugar to the Phys Ed teacher. Though Mom's gifts made the recipients feel special, her presence, friendship, and caring nature meant more to them than the physical trinkets themselves. She was a natural-born gift giver who often flexed her generosity muscles more than the average person.

Whether you're like Mom or not, there is something to be learned from the act of generosity on your *good mourning* journey. Generosity makes you feel better. It's as simple as that. Dr. Lisa Firestone, PhD explains this in her article, "Why Generosity Is Good for You." She says, *"First, it's important to note that the form of generosity that most benefits us isn't measured in a dollar amount or a physical gain. What matters is the sensitivity we offer to another person. The more directly we see our personal efforts impact someone else, the more we gain from the experience of giving."*

While we tend to focus on our own sadness and needs when we've lost someone, the best thing we can do is look outside ourselves. Being generous is a very good way to do that. According to Firestone, *"The second direct benefit we gain from giving is that generosity inherently shifts our focus off of ourselves. While it's important to maintain a healthy level of self-awareness and sensitivity to oneself, often the focus we put on ourselves is filtered through a negative lens. Many of our thoughts about ourselves are tinged with criticism, stress, doubt, uncertainty, and obsession, none of which do any good for our level of confidence and success."* [26]

I agree with Firestone, but I especially like her final point. Generosity is contagious. Once you're in action serving those around you, you're likely to continue. This ultimately creates a new generosity mindset. It did this for my dear friend, Dan Benjamin. I met him in my first futures trading class that I took with Dad. We went around the class and introduced ourselves by telling the group our "why" for wanting to earn money as traders. After hearing my desire to open a *good mourning* retreat home for fellow mourners in memory of Mom, he came up to me at the break.

"Hi, Jen, I'm Dan. I'm so sorry to hear about your mother. I could sense how much you loved her, and your '*good mourning*' house is such a wonderful idea." I could barely hold back the tears to express how much his kind words meant to me. Dan instantly knew what to do. He made me laugh by joking about his bean burger hardening to a brick in the microwave as we stood there chatting.

Dan gave me the rare gift of laughter that those of us who are in mourning struggle to find on our own. What he said next is another thing fellow mourners find comfort in. "You know, Jen, I lost my wife, Carol, five years ago to cancer. She was such a special woman, like your mother." Though I was sad to hear of his loss, I did appreciate his willingness to share. It

---

26 Firestone, Lisa. "Why Generosity Is Good for You!" Psychalive.org, www. psychalive.org/why-generosity-is-good-for-you/

showed he knew what I was going through. We talked about Carol and Mom until it was time for us to return to class.

The next day, I walked into class to find a beautiful bouquet of red roses with my name on it. I instantly looked at my father, and he shook his head. Then I saw Dan out of the corner of my eye. He smiled at me and signaled me to grab a cup of coffee with him.

"Dan, are you the one who gave me those beautiful red roses?"

"Yes, it was me. When I heard about your mom, my heart broke. I couldn't stop thinking about our conversation yesterday. And last night, I knew I had to do something to show my sympathy to you," he said.

"Dan, I cannot thank you enough," I replied.

"You're welcome, Jen. Ya know, I was a little nervous giving a young woman such a sentimental gift, but I had to. I hope you don't mind."

"Of course not," I said and thanked him again.

After the week-long class ended, Dan and I kept in touch. We talked about our trading plans but most of all, our losses. He lit up whenever he talked about Carol. I did, too. Through our talks, I learned she and Mom were uncannily similar. Though Mom was an incessant gift giver, she hated clutter. So did Carol. When Dan brought her gifts from his travels, they sat on the kitchen counter for approximately three weeks and then went straight into the garbage can.

"It was like clockwork," Dan chuckled. "She threw away almost anything, blindly. Even twelve-hundred-dollar checks!"

She'd keep every surface clear, at any cost. Even the fresh, uneaten thirty pounds of salmon Dan brought all the way from Seattle—gone in an instant. Not realizing what it was, she relocated the box off the kitchen counter and into Dan's office. (Fortunately, he found it before it went bad.) What Carol didn't throw away were opportunities to be generous to her students. In fact, she was *the* teacher every single parent on this planet wished for their son or daughter.

Carol was respected. She was loved. She was also beautiful, which put her in a situation where an eight-year-old boy conned her into helping him with his work, so he could kiss her on the cheek. But that cheap attempt to win her affection didn't rattle Carol. She simply played it off.

She played off her cancer, too, claiming her pain associated with the most debilitating disease on earth was "nothing."

"That was Carol," Dan said. When cancer took her life, he was faced with a very important decision.

Be bitter?

Or…

Be better?

It was as if his *good mourning* spirit was awakened in that moment. He knew what he had to do. He had to be better.

Dan had ministered to people as a deacon of his church for several years, but he never thought he would encounter cancer so personally. Worse, he never thought he'd encounter death from cancer. And never in a million years did he think it would be his darling Carol.

When the woman of his dreams died, Dan's generosity took another form. He no longer had the pleasure of showering Carol with gifts from his adventures. After completing his first grief program as a student at his church, he took on giving the gift of teaching it.

Just like his wife Carol did.

For the next several years, he led grief sessions for the community. Because of this selfless act, he was able to help people with their pain. "It's not easy to listen to hard things," Dan said. "I don't listen because it's easy. I just care about the person. When your heart connects with someone, you'll say things they'll be able to interpret." His heart spoke to mine that fateful day in the lobby with scents of black bean burgers in the air.

Generosity can come in all forms. It can come in little boxes of Good and Plenty. It can come in a bouquet of red roses. In Dan's case, it came in the form of a generous, loving teacher. For me, it comes in the form of gift giving. Whenever I hand a bag full of presents to someone I love, I think of Mom and how much joy she got out of making others feel special. I have a feeling Dan won't stop giving, either. He'll forever be a giver of his time for those who are in need of a gentle, caring mentor.

If you're not feeling your best right now, giving may be the last thing on your mind. I promise, if you do even the smallest act of kindness today, you will start to feel better. Here's a short list of ideas from RandomActsOfKindness.org to get the cogs rolling.[27]

1. Tell someone they dropped a dollar (even though they didn't). Then give them a dollar.
2. Surprise a neighbor with freshly baked cookies or treats!
3. Leave a gas gift card at a gas pump.
4. Place positive body image notes in jean pockets at a department store.
5. Smile at five strangers.
6. Hold up positive signs for traffic or in a park for people exercising outside!
7. Return shopping carts for people at the grocery store.
8. Leave a kind server the biggest tip you can afford.
9. Take flowers or treats to the nurses' station at your nearest hospital.
10. Tape coins around a playground for kids to find.

When you share the gift of generosity, your world is brighter, giving you room for the healing you desire.

---

27 "50 Kindness Ideas for Random Acts of Kindness Day." Randomactsof-kindness.org, www.randomactsofkindness.org/the-kindness-blog/2943-50-kindness-ideas-for-random-acts-of-kindness-day

In the next chapter, we'll learn about Michael's story of how one simple request gave him the chance to connect with his late sister.

Here's everything we've learned about the power of generosity...

GOOD MOURNING INSIGHTS

- Generosity is contagious.
- Giving helps us create a generosity mindset that helps us look outside ourselves.
- In your loss, you can choose to be bitter or to be better. Generosity is one way you can be better.

CHAPTER 13

OPENNESS—MICHAEL'S OPEN HEART

———

"Openness isn't the end; it's the beginning."

—MARGARET HEFFERNAN

I pretended I didn't hear her.

"You don't have to do this if you don't want to, you know?" Mom repeated. I sat in the driver's seat of her car, key in my hand, staring off into the distance. Tears welled in my eyes as I finally inserted the key in the ignition. To avoid her gaze, I quickly looked out the side window. There, crisp yellow leaves fell slowly from the cluster of maple trees across the lake. We sat in silence. We watched golfers move from hole to hole in their tiny green carts on the lush course.

I was jolted back to the present when I heard a car horn beep. I saw my wedding planner getting in her car. My mind drifted to the final dinner selections Mom had just helped me make.

The wedding was just a month away. I chose the chicken marsala despite Mom's fear the cutlets were too small. We continued to sit. Tears fell down my face and dripped on my jeans. Through my blurry vision, I managed to watch the clock change from 5:15 to 5:16, then 5:17. I watched it all the way to 5:27.

Mom simply waited with me.

She waited for me to make the next move or say the next word. But nothing came out. I didn't know how to tell her I was scared or that I was in too deep. The funny thing is she already knew all that. She simply grabbed my hand and said, "It will be okay, Jen." The reality was I wasn't ready. She knew it. Just like she always did. In fact, Mom could read me better than I could read myself. She had this way of being able to sense my hesitation or fear before I could. Her heart was always open that way.

I went through with the wedding and it was beautiful. I'll cherish the memory forever because my mom was there with me. My marriage, however, didn't last forever—just four years and then I decided to pull the plug. Some called me a coward, a quitter, or a failure, and that's how I felt. Mom called me nothing. She welcomed me back into her home with open arms. It was two months before I found my own place. She never once said, "I told you so."

All I got was open-hearted love. She knew that's what I needed. A mother always knows. Always. She knew when I was not "fine." She knew when I needed a hug and when I did want her advice but was too pig-headed to ask for it. She knew, period. It was part of her DNA.

Now that she's gone, I constantly wonder if she can still read or even hear my thoughts. I often wonder if she can see me or if she has any idea what I'm up to. When I started a new job a year after she died, I thought about the *Good luck! You'll do great!* text she had sent when I started my last position. The moment I realized she wasn't there to wish me luck this time, I was a bit forlorn. As I walked toward the front door, I looked down at the cigarette butts on the wet pavement, and something (or someone?) told me to pick my head up. There on the back of someone's car was a decal that read *Mama Sue*.

I couldn't believe my eyes. I took it as a message from her to wish me well on my first day. I got goosebumps on my fore-arms and a tingling throughout my body. I went from sad to glad in a heartbeat. My own logic went out the window in that millisecond because my instinct was to look around to see if she was there. She wasn't.

Or so I thought.

I had discovered that thoughts of her gave me a chance to feel her presence. I believe she knew I needed to that day. She wanted to show me "Mama Sue" was proud of me. Since then, I love to think of her and wait. All the fun is in the wait-ing, sort of like when I used to count down until Christmas morning. Now, I count down until Mom's essence shows up. It usually happens pretty quickly because she knows how impatient I am.

Another time, I was in the country. It was a gorgeous day, so I took a bike ride. The sun beat down on my head, so I looked up and closed my eyes for a moment and thought of her. Not even two seconds later, I opened them to find two beautiful red cardinals flying right in front of me.

My heart flooded with love and happiness. Mom always had a soft spot for birds and fed them year-round with seed in the front yard. It was no surprise she appeared as one of her feathery friends. That was the exact sign I needed that day. She knew it, too. She now seems to know I'm open to seeing her and feeling her presence every moment of every day. I watch for the magical moments to appear.

That's what web guru and *Ted Talk* speaker Michael Tesalona did.

When his larger-than-life sister, Nina, died suddenly in a car wreck, he was in total disbelief. He had lost his best friend. It was just before Thanksgiving, 2016. As he stood over her at the wake one final time, he didn't say his goodbyes. He knew in his heart her death wasn't really the end. When it came time for Michael to close her casket, he did something that would change the trajectory of his *good mourning* journey.

He simply prayed to her, *"Nina, I want to see you again. Let me see you again. Please let me see you again."*

Later that weekend, he and his family were on their way to their traditional after-Thanksgiving movie that they knew Nina wouldn't want them to forego. Michael hung back in the lobby as the rest stopped for popcorn.

That's when he saw her out of the corner of his eye. He could swear it was Nina. It had to be her. Had he not just laid his precious sister to rest he would have said it *was* her. Her beautiful brown locks were tucked back behind diamond-adorned ears as a smirk passed on her youthful, innocent face. Her soulful brown eyes shot a beam right through his heart as he instantly thought she had come back to life. She raised a perfectly manicured eyebrow, as if questioning whether he was going to come talk to her. As he attempted to walk toward this mysterious woman, a sea of people swarmed in.

Nina was among the crowds, as she always was. That's where she felt most comfortable, after all. A distant but fond memory flashed through Michael's mind of when she came to stay with him in Spain. When he would lose sight of her, all he had to do was listen for signs of laughter. That's how he would find her. She was always surrounded by groups of people in awe of her hilarity and charm as she effortlessly cracked them up. He often found people wanting to hold onto her. Her beautiful *"light side"* was so intoxicating, they wanted to drink it all up like sangria.

Michael would force his way into the center where he found her laughing joyfully along with them and gently whisper in her ear, "Okay, Nina, it's time to go home now." She always trusted her big brother, so she didn't put up a fight. She let go of them, so she went, but not before she said goodbye to everyone.

All of a sudden in the theater lobby, Michael came out of his Nina trance. He had heard his name being called from a distance. "Michael! It's time to go in now," his family beckoned.

He looked over to see his uncanny Nina look-a-like at the ticket booth, standing right there in front of all his family. They didn't even notice her.

"I'll be right there," he replied. He lingered to catch a longer glimpse of this woman who resembled his sister to a T. He wanted to ingrain this spitting image of Nina into his brain, but most of all, into his heart. Little did he know at the time, he didn't have to do that, not even one bit. After this magical moment, Nina began showing up everywhere he went. It was almost like the time she appeared in his kitchen in Spain all those years ago.

Every time he thinks he sees her or hears her laugh now, he looks up and smiles. For him, it's like she never left. Everywhere he goes, she goes, too. As he and his family approach her five-year death anniversary, he loves to play hide and seek with Nina every day. He simply makes the request, *"Nina, let me see you today."* Like clockwork, she appears.

As you venture out into the world today, I challenge you to do this. Ask for your loved one to show themselves to you in some way. If it doesn't happen right away, don't get discouraged. Sometimes all it takes is a simple thought. You will be pleasantly surprised, just as Michael and I were, to discover that your loved one really isn't gone.

Before I saw such miraculous signs that Mom was near me, I really wasn't open to the fact of seeing her again in my lifetime. I was happily mistaken when she proved me wrong. She continues to prove me wrong to this day.

One of Mom's favorite movies of all time was *The Sound of Music*. She often quoted the main character, Maria: "When God closes a door, He always opens a window." While the door on her life has closed, a window has opened my heart to the possibility of seeing her every day.

Knowing that simple, comforting fact will do wonders for you on your own *good mourning* journey. Most of all, seeing a familiar smile at the movies can suddenly give you the power to wear one of your own.

In the next chapter, we'll learn about Gigi's story of how her creativity sparked one of her life's newest passions.

First, let's take a look at the things we've learned from this chapter...

GOOD MOURNING INSIGHTS
- Be open to the possibility of seeing your loved one again. They will take care of the rest.
- When you ask for them to show themselves to you, you'll be surprised at how quickly they can appear.
- Play hide and seek with them, looking for their presence wherever you go.
- If you need a little extra inspiration, Michael appeared on a grief-themed *Ted Talk* called "Leave Your Light On."[28]

---

28 Tesalona, Michael. "Leave Your Light On; Compassion in a Time of Grief." Ted.com, https://www.ted.com/talks/michael_tesalona_leave_your_light_on_compassion_in_a_time_of_grief

CHAPTER 14

ORIGINALITY—GIGI'S MOTHER OF ALL IDEAS

—

*"It is better to fail in originality than
to succeed in imitation."*

—HERMAN MELVILLE

I had to be different.

Always.

It was in my blood.

Halloween was the time for me to test out my silly creativity.
The nuttier the idea, the better. The mere thought of being
a humdrum black cat or a boring witch haunted me. Mom
knew it, too. She knew how much I strived to find the most
original costume every single year. She was the same. I loved
hearing about her dress-up escapades when she was a kid,
and I drew on her creations for inspiration.

While I did love to come up with my own ideas, there was something about Mom's. They were always perfect. *Always.* Like the year she suggested I be an Old Maid from the card game. I stuffed my shirt with towels, wrapped a pillow around my rump and covered my padded body with a wool skirt and blouse from a secondhand store. Essentially, I was the child version of Mrs. Doubtfire. I thought this costume was, hands down, the magnum opus of my life. But the next year had to be even better.

Thanks to Mom, it was. As I was doing my math homework, she happened to notice my list of "Halloween Costume Ideas" next to me. She noticed not much was written down. She pretended to mind her own business but couldn't resist jumping in.

"How about a clown?" she proposed.

"No, Jesse was that last year."

"I know. I know. How about a scientist?"

"No, too boring," I said.

I tapped my pencil on my notebook, waiting for the next brilliant idea to exit her lips. "I got it! I got it! How about the Absent-Minded Professor?" she exclaimed, as if her two previous ideas mated and had a Halloween costume baby.

It sounded funny, but I was only nine and didn't have a clue what it was. Noticing my puzzlement, she explained, "You know, a goofy scientist with the crazy hair and glasses. What do you think?"

It was the exact idea I was searching for.

"Dad could get a lab coat from work and you can use his old briefcase," she said.

"Thanks, Mom!" I ran over to give her a huge hug and then flew downstairs to tell my sisters. "Guess what Mom just came up with for my costume? An absent-minded professor!" After revealing my now sacred idea, I begged them not to tell anyone at school. My costume was on a strictly "need to know" basis. I didn't want anyone stealing it.

The next day, I came home from school to find a collection of costume props lined up on my bed. There was a handmade *"Harvard or Bust"* sign on a piece of blank computer paper, a curly sky-blue wig, and a pair of round glasses with distorted lenses. It was hard to contain my excitement. I threw down my book bag and began to try everything on. Admiring my epic transformation in the mirror, I was ecstatic at how goofy I looked.

Mom knocked on the door and said, "Jen, I got you one more thing for your absent-minded professor costume." She pulled a bag from behind her back, and inside was a pair of wonky, crooked, yellow buck teeth.

I ripped open the package and put them in my mouth.

What Mom said next was priceless, "Jen, you look like a million bucks." (Now, you know where I get my love for puns.) Not only did I look it, I felt it, too.

When the Halloween Parade at school began, I was so proud. In my mind, I had the most original costume, and Mom was the one who helped me come up with it. She was waving at me when my class marched by her in the hallway on our way to the gym. I couldn't hold back my smile, not realizing that sudden movement would make my ill-fitting buck teeth fall out. She laughed out loud and quickly covered her mouth, and, as if on cue, so did I at the exact same time.

That funny incident marked a special moment for Mom and me. As I thought about it decades later, I realized that she and I spoke the same silly language, especially the way we bonded over off-the-wall Halloween costumes.

When I met Gigi Trencher for the first time, she told me all about the unique connection she and her mother, Vanna, shared. For them, it was what all girls love—clothes and jewelry.

As a young girl, Gigi remembers her mother, the "flea hunter" going from antique store to antique store in their hometown of Potomac, Maryland. Vanna's mission was always to find the perfect accompaniment for her latest ensemble. No matter what it was, Vanna always knew what she was looking for. "It could have been an emerald-green brooch to match her gown or a pair of costume chandelier earrings to go with her custom-made Thai dress," said Gigi. "She stopped at nothing to find the right piece."

If Vanna couldn't find what she was looking for, she would design it herself. Gigi loved watching her mother's brain work as she created her own jewelry on their trips to Bangkok. "Her imagination had no limits," Gigi said. "My mother was a visionary. She started with the jewelry and then created the perfect dress to match. Her process was magical." Gigi especially loved that Vanna asked the seamstresses to make child-sized versions of the dresses for her. "We'd come out of the fitting room as all the women in our family took shots of us like paparazzi."

Feminine beauty was always very important to her mother. When the harsh exposure to chemo and radiation ravaged her skin, Gigi went on an intense search to find a skincare line for her mother that would work for cancer patients. She came up empty. What she did next was reminiscent of her mother's creative spirit. She took on designing the skincare brand herself. As of this writing, she was in the process of working with a number of oncologists, doctors and dermatologists to create one for her mother as she continued her treatment.

But that's not all Gigi's creating...

Another project near and dear to her heart is something called "Final Conversations." Having trouble navigating the delicate conversations surrounding death, she wants to humanize the process and the conversations. "I want to help the dying and their loved ones by giving them a respectful, comfortable way to have these final conversations," she said. She is designing a curriculum that outlines every possible question that needs to be answered, from last wishes to funeral arrangements.

Gigi credits her creation of both these projects to the connection she has with her mother. When she saw a void, she filled it, just like her mother did years ago in the jewelry and clothing shops of Bangkok. "These are the projects that are important to me. They represent my mother perfectly. I love that what I'm doing aligns with the woman I'll always love," she said.

Like Gigi, my heart has led me to do bigger and better things in my mom's memory. When I lost her, my quirky brain started churning again. I felt a yearning to exercise the creative bone Mom bestowed upon me, even if my ideas are a bit unconventional. Not having her to bounce them off of, I had to tap into the eternal silly bond we share. The idea I've landed on not only represents the selfless, caring woman Mom was but also showcases her vibrant, goofy side.

If you've ever seen the movie *Elf*, with Will Ferrell, you'll know his character, Buddy, delivers his estranged father a "Christmas Gram." Though this will undoubtedly be a logistical nightmare, I want to do the same thing for mourners. I'll call it a "Happiness Gram." With a brief doorstep-delivered song, I want to spread cheer by singing loudly for all to hear. Though this idea needs to incubate for a while, I'm going to continue to perfect it. I know Mom will be cheering me on and giggling at me from the sidelines.

The one thing I encourage you to take from Gigi's story is to be as original as you can be when it comes to mourning. Your ideas can be wacky like mine or sweet like Gigi's. Whatever they are, they are yours. Here's what's really special: nothing and no one can take them from you.

In the next chapter, we'll learn about Carrie's story of how one act of courage challenged her to do the one thing she feared the most.

First, here's what we've learned...

GOOD MOURNING INSIGHTS

- Think of a silly or sweet idea and share it with the world.
- Remember the little things you shared with your lost loved one and cherish that unique connection.
- Try on being goofy, just for the sake of it. You may just make yourself laugh.
- If all else fails, go to your closet and try on silly things you find there. Pretend it's Halloween and go trick-or-treat your neighbor.

CHAPTER 15

DETERMINATION— CARRIE'S BABY STEPS

———

"Ring the bells that still can ring, forget your perfect offering, there is a crack in everything, that's how the light gets in."

—LEONARD COHEN

She called him Charry.

He was five feet tall and skinny as a rail. No one in our family gave him a second look. Not Mom. She walked right over and picked him up out of a pile of brush. In her attempt to dust the soot off him, Mom managed to get more on herself. She didn't care. She needed his strength, ash or no ash, to get her up the mountain.

The truth was Mom's knees were weak. So weak, in fact, they gave out unexpectedly, causing her to stumble. Her wobbly, foal-like stance was not going to get in the way of her see-ing St. Mary's Falls. That's when she decided to commission Charry, her beloved walking stick, to give her and her knees a break. This stick's name matched his "charred" exterior, the result of being burned in a forest fire that had ravaged Glacier Park in the summer of 2016.

When our family approached the trailhead, Mom peered into the faraway distance. "It's a long way up there, huh?" she asked rhetorically. She knew the answer. No matter how far it was, it was going to be a long way for her.

Dad answered, "It's 1.7 miles one way. If you want, I can stay behind…"

Not letting him finish, she interjected, "No! I'm going to see these falls."

He signaled her to go first, holding her hand as she stepped up onto the first rock.

This was not a smooth paved trail. Not only was it covered in jagged rocks, but we had to cross streams and hop over big gaping holes. Mom felt every step. I knew because I watched her wince in pain as she made her way. It was hard for me to see her struggle, so I went ahead. Dad, however, stayed close by her side just in case. She knew what he was doing, but she didn't want help.

All she wanted was to reach the top.

What I loved most about Mom's intrepid trek up the mountain was her high spirits. If she hadn't had a walking stick or a noticeable limp, you would never have known she was hurting. She told jokes and poked fun at herself and her new timber friend, but not once did she complain about her ailing knees. I'd run back to check on her from time to time. "Mom, how are you doing?" I asked.

"Oh, just fine, Jen. I'm the happy little caboose," she would reply with a wry smile.

"We're almost there. You can do it," I encouraged.

"You don't have to tell me. I'm doing it," she said.

And she did.

At the top of the falls, she had the biggest smile on her face. It was so big, in fact, I commemorated the moment with a photo, now a cherished keepsake of mine. Mom never said it, but you could tell how proud she was of herself for pushing through the agony of her aching knees. The glory she celebrated at her accomplishment was worth every ounce of pain she endured.

In mourning the loss of a loved one, you also have to push through the pain of grief. When you do, you have a sense of renewed strength from within available to you. It can redefine your life and true purpose if you let it.

That's what Carrie Brady did. She trudged through her loss and came out a stronger woman because of it. While her story isn't for the faint of heart, she not once lost hope. Not when she found out her soon-to-be adopted baby girl was addicted to methadone. Not when she got the call that the baby was life-flighted to intensive care. Not after the ten-day-old baby died in Carrie's arms in the newborn intensive care unit (NICU). And not even weeks later when the mother blamed Carrie for the baby's tragic death.

Not once.

Carrie's saving grace was... grace. Grace from God, grace from her family, grace from herself. She muscled through her grief or, as she described it, she "ninja-slopped through it" because "there was no other way." After she gave away the stroller, the onesies, and every trace of a baby she could find in her home, she and her family ventured to their lake house for a few days for a much-needed escape.

The peaceful lake was the perfect backdrop for her grief, but Carrie discovered that the power of true healing could only be found *inside* the house. She surrounded herself with boundless, soul-giving joy that only children can bring. While it may seem completely illogical for Carrie to spend her days playing dress-up and sleeping in bunk beds alongside her nieces, they ultimately healed her broken heart. "The way they were so present in every moment snapped me right out of my sorrow, my nightmares, and my early-morning bouts of endless tears," she said.

In that moment, she knew what she had to do. Instead of burying her grief, she found the courage within to try adoption again. Her inner fortitude had been there all along, allowing her to start to have a *good mourning*. After much prayer and reflection, she made the call. Little did she know she would be matched with another drug-dependent mother. Though her friends and family pleaded with her not to go through another gut-wrenching adoption, she felt called to be a mother.

Carrie was determined to remain strong but at times felt a bit hopeless. That's when she got down on her knees and prayed to her little girl—the one she lost in the NICU. Carrie admitted, "I would have probably given up if it hadn't been for that little girl," who she now calls her guardian angel. Her guardian angel guided her all the way into young Grayson's heart.

He became Carrie's adopted son on January 7, 2019. The moment he was born, "I held him and never put him down until we left the NICU two weeks later," she said. Their stay was extended to ensure Grayson was properly weaned from his meth addiction. Now, with his love flowing through her veins, she can't imagine life without him. "He and I were meant to be a part of each other's lives," she said.

When tragedy strikes, our inclination is to let fear take over. Carrie could have succumbed to her trepidation after losing her first baby. If she had, she would not have met Grayson or become his loving mother. She maintained her positive, courageous outlook every day, just as we all must to get through the hard times.

Once, when I was at my wits' end with my mother's death, one of the most unassuming and beautiful experiences of my life happened in the last place on earth I would have expected.

I found myself in a dingy public bathroom at Penn Station in New York City. I reached for the faucet to wash my hands. There, beside each sink, were those dreaded motion-sensor soap dispensers. I tried three out of the four but could not retrieve an ounce of suds.

I looked up to find an old woman at the fourth station. She greeted me with a warm smile. As I asked her if she had any soap, I realized we didn't speak the same language. What she did next gave me a chill down my spine. She gently took my dirty hand and put it underneath her dispenser. As it dropped a dollop of soap, she smiled at me and gave my arm a warm tug and then went on her way.

Something magical happened in that exchange of kindness and warmth. The fear spell that had overtaken my life after Mom died finally broke—for good. Though no words were spoken, I could feel this stranger's unconditional love, renewing my strength again.

It takes courage and strength to stay on a love-filled path, but it's worth the trouble. In love my mom and Carrie's little girl live on. Or should I say they "love" on? That's worth living for. If you do anything today, spread love wherever you go. When you give love, it comes back to you. Most of all, love provides us the strength we need to press on.

In the next chapter, we'll discover how Spencer uses the art of music to keep his father's memory alive.

First, let's review all that we've learned…

GOOD MOURNING **INSIGHTS**

- Spread love as often as you can each and every day to renew your strength and ward off fear.
- When you push through the agony of grief, you may discover your own inner strength on the other side.
- Grace can come from an old woman washing your hands, from watching little children play, or anywhere you allow yourself to be open to it.

CHAPTER 16

MEMORIES—SPENCER'S COUNTRY LIVING

---

*"Memory... is the diary that we
all carry about with us."*

—OSCAR WILDE

My balloon didn't merely *pop*...

It disintegrated.

The tiny pieces of the imaginary latex confetti floated above my head as Mom announced the most unacceptable news possible, "Jennifer, you are only thirteen years old and you are NOT going to that concert alone." My life was officially over. To be seen within one hundred yards of Mom as I saw Blink 182, *the* hottest punk band of my middle-school years, meant nothing short of social annihilation.

Once her mind was made up, there was no reasoning with her. I bolted to my room and slammed the door so hard it nearly fell off the hinges. Next, I switched on my boom box and played "Adam's Song," my favorite Blink 182 track, at the loudest decibel ever. It was loud enough that I could feel the vibrations in my chest. I wanted Mom to "appreciate" it all the way upstairs. I was so distraught, I could only belly-flop on my bed and bury my head in the pillow.

I'd be the laughingstock of my peers. None of *their* mothers were going to the concert. I had to do something. There was no way this could actually become a reality. I thought and thought as I cried and got black mascara all over my comforter. Then, it hit me. I jumped up and started writing down all the reasons why Mom didn't have to go.

1. *My friend, Megan, is going with me...*
2. *The concert venue workers are adults...*
3. *There will be people everywhere...*

Reasons in hand, I ran back up the stairs and begged her to let me go unsupervised. None of them worked. I could not have convinced her with five million reasons. She was going whether I liked it or not.

When the day of the concert arrived, I wanted to stay home. I didn't want to tell Megan my mom was going to the concert with us. After we picked her up, I racked my brain to figure out how to lose Mom in the crowd. That's when it came to me. I would pretend I had to go to the bathroom really bad. That way Megan and I could find our own spot without Mom trailing behind us. It was genius. I leaned over to whisper my plan in Megan's ear, and Mom eyed me in the rear-view mirror. She was onto me with her "mother radar."

The moment she put the car in park, I blurted out "Mom, I've gotta go to the bathroom REALLY bad. Megan and I are going to go ahead. We'll meet you inside the gate, okay?"

"Um, Jennifer, hold on a second. I've gotta get the chairs…"

We were already out of the car and on a tear. We stopped for a breather. "Okay, we lost Mom," I cheered. "Just make sure she can't find us inside."

"Gimme my ticket," Megan asked.

"I thought you had them!" I exclaimed.

Defeated, we slow-walked back to the car and my mom and the chairs. (The worst part was, by the time we rendezvoused with Mom, I really DID have to pee.) When we finally arrived at the gate, Mom began shuffling in her fanny pack for the tickets as Megan and I watched our young comrades go in left and right unaccompanied by their dweeby parents. I looked back over to Mom and noticed she had worn an old hat with a sweat-stained ring around the bill, the one she put on to do outside chores. It was like she was going out of her way to embarrass me.

After she handed us our tickets, we fought our way through the long lines of teenagers. Security checked her fanny pack and then showed us where the lawn seats were. We found a bare spot in between two groups of girls and put our chairs and blanket down.

"Jenny…" said Mom. I cringed when I heard her call me that, signaling to everyone I was still a child. She continued, "I'm going to be right behind you and Megan over by that tree." She pointed up the hill. I immediately turned toward the stage and tried to forget she was there.

Megan and I passed the time picking out cute boys and playing "Never Have I Ever." Then, suddenly, the infamous notes Blink played at the beginning of "Adam's Song" rang out. The crowd went wild. Before we knew it, the curtains went up, and our eyes were drawn to the top of the stage where we saw the coolest, or I should say, the hottest thing I had ever seen.

It was a gigantic sign with four massive letters, as big across as my whole backyard and engulfed in flames. It defiantly proclaimed one thing and one thing only: FU**. You get the picture.

My inner rebel was awakened. Goosebumps appeared all over my forearms. My favorite band was not only playing my favorite song but now I was experiencing visual nirvana. Nodding my head to the song, I closed my eyes and began tapping my feet. I was on top of the world. Then, my eyes shot open.

Mom!

Before I turned around to gauge her reaction, I hoped she had gone to the bathroom. Or maybe she went to buy an overpriced soft pretzel. Or perhaps there was a chance she hadn't seen the massive flaming profanity. Nope. None of the above. She stood there in complete disgust. We locked eyes. It was as if she had peered into the depths of my soul to give it a good, hard spanking when she mouthed, "Great… Jennifer."

I was mortified, embarrassed, and probably a bit ashamed because this memory has stuck with me. Ultimately, she hated the concert, but it remains one of my favorite memories of her because she sacrificed her time and sanity by going with me. At the time, it was awkward, but it has made me laugh for years. It also delights me to know the lengths she took to keep me safe.

When our loved ones die, we may want to suppress memories like this the moment they reappear in our minds. We believe we're doing ourselves a favor by sweeping them under the rug. We hide every little item that reminds us of our loved one to save ourselves from the extra suffering. Sometimes it helps, and sometimes it doesn't.

My dear friend, Bill Spencer, whom I like to call just Spencer, mourns the loss of his dad, Marlan, who was fond of referring to himself as "the Old Sarge." (Marlan was a New York City police sergeant for fifteen years.)

Spencer preserves the memories he has and visits with them often, the way you visit favorite songs from summers long ago. He relives them in a way that helps him mourn and connect with his dad. He has dedicated himself to this as a daily practice. Because of that, he's able to recount, in near-perfect detail, memories of his dad that go back nearly fifty years.

After I shared my first concert experience with Spencer, he was over the moon with excitement to share his, too. His dad had tagged along, but more as a necessity considering Spencer was just six years old. Unlike Mom, Sarge really wanted to hear the concert with his son that chilly October evening back in 1969. The place? Symphony Hall in Newark, New Jersey. The headliner? Country music legend Johnny Cash.

"The Old Sarge" lived and breathed country music. He had primed Spencer early for his love for Johnny Cash. There were the impromptu jam sessions where he loved hearing his dad play Johnny's hit, "Give My Love to Rose" for him and his family.

Sarge noticed Spencer's love of the music and signed him up for guitar lessons. He was a natural player, just like his dad. It didn't take long for Spencer to master every Johnny Cash song he learned.

When Sarge learned that Johnny was coming to town for a concert, he sent away for tickets. Spencer was beside himself with joy when Sarge broke the good news. He would ask his father every chance he got, "Did you get the tickets yet?" Spencer even remembers the tickets were light blue when they finally arrived in the mail. The night of the concert, Sarge took a detour to the town diner for a special dinner, followed by Spencer's favorite hot chocolate with marshmallows.

He remembers entering the auditorium and being in awe at its grandeur. The seats, the carpet, and the curtains were a deep and luxurious red. Their seats were good, just a few rows back from the stage. Tommy Cash and The Statler Brothers warmed the audience up with note-perfect versions of "Six White Horses" and "Flowers on the Wall."

Finally, the big red curtain was drawn. Spencer sat in awe of the massive sparkling gold sign that hovered above the stage courtesy of radio station WJRZ "the only country in the city." (His retelling of this Oz-like vision made me think of my "flaming surprise" at the Blink 182 concert.)

Even more magical, the gorgeous, crisp, clear sounds of the band had him hypnotized. "It was like hearing a waterfall for the first time," he said. Spencer remembers seeing a white spotlight shine on a lone figure dressed in black with slicked-back hair and a guitar draped across his back. This distinctive silhouette was none other than Johnny Cash, live and in-person... and larger than life.

After finishing his biggest hit song, "Folsom Prison Blues," the great man uttered his signature greeting, "Hello, I'm Johnny Cash." Spencer's memories of the whole thing are rich: Johnny pulling a harmonica out of his back pocket and launching into "Orange Blossom Special;" the string of songs that followed one after the other, causing Spencer to fall even more in love with not only Johnny's playing but with country music. Johnny didn't leave the stage until he had played all his hits, including "Jackson" "Ring of Fire," "A Boy Named Sue," and "Walk the Line."

Sarge bought Spencer the concert booklet to keep as a memento. The moment he got home, he cut it up and pasted the pictures all over his wall. His first concert experience was memorialized all over his room.

That first concert was just one of many musical outings Spencer and his dad would share in the coming years. In fact, they took in shows by all the leading country stars of the era. Buck Owens, Porter Wagoner with Dolly Parton, George Jones, Loretta Lynn, Tammy Wynette, Waylon Jennings, Willie Nelson, and Merle Haggard. They saw them all, and Spencer remembers every one of the glorious hours he and his dad spent together.

The sounds of those shows spawned a new love for Spencer. While he enjoyed the singing, harmonica, and acoustic guitar playing, he became infatuated with the bass guitar. Again, his father took notice. He bought Spencer his first bass guitar, which Spencer laughingly calls "a short-sale piece of crap." He loved it, though, mainly because his father had gotten it for him. The first song he ever learned was "Smoke on the Water" which he later played at his first gig. Naturally, his biggest fan, the Old Sarge, came to watch Spencer every chance he got, establishing a one-man posse for him and his band.

His father wanted a piece of the action, too. Sarge bought a bass guitar, and even though he had been a self-taught musician his entire life to this point, Sarge broke down and took guitar lessons at the ripe old age of sixty-two. He did it so he could play music with his only son. They played together for years and only stopped when Sarge became too sick and weak.

That didn't stop their musical connection. To keep their shared affinity for country music alive, they watched The Highwaymen, a country supergroup fronted by their beloved Johnny Cash. Sarge loved the songs, and that made Spencer love them even more. "The last thing we did together was watch that show for the 500th time," Spencer said. "It will always hold a special place in my heart."

When Sarge died, Spencer was heartbroken. But he knew retiring his bass and his love for country music wasn't an option. He embraced the memories openly. Playing the bass and listening to country music every chance he gets allows him to feel his father close by. He even shares his father's favorite tunes with me.

We're both ardent country music fans, and in his weekly "Tuesday Tune" emails, Spencer allows me to enjoy and experience the songs Sarge held dear to his heart.

What I love about Spencer's story is that his memories with his father don't stay tucked away in some dusty filing cabinet in his mind. He doesn't suppress them but welcomes them as opportunities to reconnect with Sarge now that he's gone. By making his memories a mainstay in his daily life, Spencer is able to share with the world the musical gifts he cultivated with his father on his *good mourning* journey.

I don't plan to become a punk rock artist anytime soon in order to relive my first concert memory. However, I like the idea of embarrassing my son or daughter one day at their first concert, just as much as Mom did to me. I'll plan to have my dirty baseball cap and fanny pack at the ready when the time comes.

When we reminisce, tell, and relive our memories of our loved ones, it causes a ripple effect where more and more memories flood to our minds. While we may want to suppress them,

I've learned they can give us more and more opportunities to bring our loved ones back to life—again and again.

In the next chapter, we'll learn about my dear friend Natalie's story of how she taps into her natural-born gifts from her father to bring happiness into her life and to the lives of others.

Let's first take a moment to see what we've gotten in this chapter...

GOOD MOURNING INSIGHTS

- Sharing memories of our loved ones can ensure they stick with us forever.
- Reliving old times can bring us joy and give us opportunities to keep our loved ones alive.
- Remembering our young and enduring memories with our loved one can give us a sense of how they helped us be who we are.

CHAPTER 17

OSMOSIS—
NATALIE'S NIGHT IN
SHINING ARMOR

——

"The apple doesn't fall far from the tree."

—GERMAN PROVERB

She smelled her arm.

Not candles. Not roses. Not cookies.

Her arm.

What made this quirky habit of Mom's even weirder was that she *only* did it while on the phone. Her arm wouldn't come up the moment she lifted the spiral-corded receiver off the wall, though. It took the right amount of salacious gossip, mixed with high-pitched cackling, before the smelling began.

The moment her nose hit her wrist, she would often make her way up and down her arm as if she were nibbling on a cob of corn. Other times, when she was really concentrating on the subject matter, she was a bit more subtle. Then she'd let her nose hover right above the top of her wrist like a secret agent whispering covert messages into a tiny walkie talkie.

Regardless of her nose's mood that day, she made every whiff count. Each breath she took seemed to help her register tidbits of information in her brain. She picked up what was important, like a bee sensing nearby pollen deposits with its antennae. After each intake of air, she'd blurt out a signal the data was received in the form of long, drawn-out, successive words like "Right, right, right," culminated with a little chuckle.

Her artistic inhalation was never loud. She could never have been mistaken for an excited hound dog hot on a scent. No way. If she had, she would have scared off whoever she was talking to. No, her smelling had to be as inaudible as possible.

It was noticeable, however, to her nosy middle daughter who always got a kick out of watching her play the arm harmonica. Nosy. That's the operative word in this scenario. Though I never partook in the rather peculiar nasal acrobatics like dear Mom, I have the ability to smell everything under the sun. My sniffer is so powerful I smell things I don't want to smell. I can pick out a scent so obscure, so faint local mutts often bark up my tree for tips.

When Mom died, I never in a million years would have imagined I'd find myself surveying my own extremities with the old sniffer. Never. Well, I've come to discover the apple *truly* doesn't fall from the tree.

Typically, I'm a pacer when I'm on the phone. I do more loops around my home than a stock car in The Indy 500. Because of the record speed I keep, I don't have time to stop and smell the… arms. This day, however, I did. As I was talking with my Aunt Mary, I paused on the track for a moment. I was hanging on her every word and didn't want to lose sight of what she was telling me. All of a sudden, my arm came up to my nose and, like that, I gave it a sniff.

I was so caught off guard by this foreign behavior, I stopped mid-conversation. It was as if Mom herself had come into my living room and pulled my arm up to my nose like a puppeteer. I don't know if I learned this through osmosis or if it was bestowed on me in the womb. I don't have a clue what it is with Mom and me and the smelling of the arms, but it's a thing.

And now, it's a beautiful thing that reminds me of her. My smelling antics made me smile so much that day, I now do it just to do it. I don't have to be on the phone, either. I do it while reading a book, watching TV, or cooking. With every sniff, it's like I'm breathing my mother's presence back into my life somehow. Before I begin, I always make sure the blinds are closed in case anyone's watching.

Surprise discoveries like these can be very comforting. Physical signs like a visit from a cardinal or butterfly can have us believe our loved ones' spirits are nearby. We can also wait for and pay attention to our little "osmosis moments."

Whether you're related to the person who has died or not, you can still enjoy experimenting with their trademarks—the habits or behaviors that were distinctively theirs. You may choose to try their favorite peanut butter and pickle sandwich for lunch one day or wear yellow socks just like they used to in a superstitious effort to ward off bad weather. Whatever it is, these are the small choices we can make every day to help us laugh off our hurt while we honor the ones we've lost.

My dear friend and author of *The Language of Loss*, Natalie Sanchez, and her dad, Paul, definitely came from the same mold. She and Paul were quintessential night owls. Growing up watching him run to Walgreens for his favorite bagel bite midnight snack or, maybe, play the drums at 1 a.m., Natalie quickly learned and adopted her dad's nocturnal ways.

"Being a night person has become ingrained in me. For as long as I can remember, I would find myself staying up as late as I could watching documentaries with my dad. His favorites were the conspiracy theories," Natalie chuckled. "He was fascinated by the flat earth theory. Elvis conspiracy theories, too. No matter the topic, he got sucked into them."

And it followed that so did Natalie. Paul got her to believe the age-old adage, "Don't believe everything you're told," which is a principle she lives by to this day. What she does believe in is sharing her late father's many qualities with the world. "We've always been similar, but after he died, I felt the need to emulate him even more," she said. Well, maybe not his late-night bagel bite making, but she's made it a personal mission of hers to continue his most beloved passion of music.

He passed away unexpectedly from a stroke on March 9, 2018. Natalie remembers approaching her father as he lay still in the hospital bed. She wasn't afraid at all as she sat on the bedside stool, gently picking up his hand and holding it. She wanted to immortalize the feeling of his hand in her memory forever. As she thought, *This will be the last time I touch him, but it certainly won't be the last my dad will touch me, and countless others, with his gift of music.*

Like Mozart or Beethoven, some people are born gifted musicians. They don't need to practice or work at it. Hand them an instrument, any instrument, for that matter, and music just flows out. Paul was one of those people. He played every instrument ever created by human hands—guitar, drums, piano, ukulele, trumpet… you name it. He played it and he played it stupendously well.

Paul was also an avid follower of classic rock. "Whenever he'd play Tom Petty, The Beatles, or The Police, I'd think, *That's his music.*" After he died, Natalie felt differently. "When my dad was gone and his music was still here, I realized how much his music impacted me," she said. That's when she decided to sift through his wide collection of songs from his favorite bands to make her now "Hearing Him Through Music" playlist encompassing over three hundred of Paul's most cherished jams.

Because music made up the fabric of Paul's life, Natalie made sure the notes never stopped despite the loss of her father. When she got home from the hospital, she grabbed the ukulele her father gave her a few years before and just started plucking. She really hadn't a clue what she was doing, but she "was determined to play it, no matter what." This bold stunt gave her the confidence to brave her fears of singing her dad's favorite song, "Edelweiss," from his all-time favorite movie, *The Sound of Music*, at the funeral in front of friends and family.

By then, she was on a roll. Given Paul was an adept writer, Natalie felt more passionate about her writing than ever before. She crafted a eulogy as well as a poem for the back of the prayer cards that funeral-goers could take home as keepsakes. "These are two things I never thought I'd have the courage to do," Natalie said humbly. What's so impressive about the super-talented Natalie is that she accomplished both extremely well.

Once her pen and quill were out, she couldn't put them away. Following in the footsteps of her creative mastermind father, it was only natural for Natalie to meld his two most beloved pastimes into one. That's when her songwriting was born. After gleaning inspiration from her dad's favorite song, "When the Day Is Done" by The Samples, the lyrics began to flow out of her.

She finished a few songs and then shared her creations with her uncles, also very talented musicians like their brother. Ironically, they had been doing the exact same thing—writing and composing songs for Paul. The rest of the album they named "For Our Superman" came together like magic for their Superman-T-shirt-wearing hero. The Sanchez family album features amazingly beautiful songs commemorating Paul's life.

"Losing a parent helps us become the person we're meant to be," Natalie said boldly. The person Natalie was meant to be is a fearless songwriter, ukulele- and guitar-plucking virtuoso, and the author of *The Language of Loss*, where she features stories, just like hers, of people on this path of self-discovery after loss.

Though Paul wasn't around to see her complete her final manuscript, he showed up with a late-night bite in the library. While typing away, Natalie's mouth gravitated down to the collar of her T-shirt. So enthralled with the story she was bringing to life, she subconsciously grabbed it with her teeth and started chomping away. "I was so shocked at what had just happened, I sent a picture to my Mom titled '*Look what I was doing!*'"

That's because her dad *always* bit the top of his T-shirt. Always. He bit it while watching TV. He did it sitting in his favorite recliner. He chomped as he clicked through emails. He even had regular biting sessions in bed before drifting off to sleep. He *always* bit his shirt. Just like he'll always live in Natalie's little osmosis moments like this, and in the many talents they share.

We're not all natural-born prodigies like Natalie. She's quite an impressive superhuman like her dad. If you're thinking you'll never be able to write songs or play the ukulele to honor your loved one, don't give it another thought. That's because the gifts you use to honor your loved one can be as simple as a laugh.

Mine was, actually.

One night, I was out with my friends and one of them tickled my funny bone so much that I cocked my head back and let out a big, hearty belly laugh—one that would make Santa, "Mr. Bowl Full of Jelly" himself jealous.

Out of nowhere, one friend said, "Jen, you laugh just like your mom."

The rest is history.

Not even two months later, I became an official Laughter Yoga Leader. Yes, that's a thing. I first heard about laughter therapy from my older sister, Amanda, but when I discovered I laugh like Mom, I pursued it. After googling "Laughter Therapy Baltimore," I was introduced to the world of Laughter Yoga and one of the most joyful spirits I've ever met, Lameteria Hall. She taught me the countless ways our bodies can benefit from long bouts of forced, even fake, laughter. Because of this training, I am now able to help others restore their bodies and joyful spirits from the art and practice of Laughter Yoga. Plus, it allows me to share Mom's laugh with the world.

If laughing isn't your thing, don't worry. Keep your eyes peeled and your ears perked because the perfect "osmosis moment" for you and your *good mourning* journey could be right around the corner.

In the next chapter, we'll learn about Jennifer's story of gumption as she found her own unique path.

First, let's get a whiff of what we've learned…

GOOD MOURNING INSIGHTS

- Sometimes we find our osmosis moments and other times they find us.
- Losing a parent, or someone close to us, allows us to become the people we're meant to be in this world.
- Nothing is ever too weird not to share or experience if it makes you feel happy and connected to your loved one.
- Arm smelling and T-shirt biting should be official Olympic sports.

CHAPTER 18

UNIQUENESS— JENNIFER'S WATERING WHOLE

———

"I personally like being unique. I like being my own person with my own style and my own opinions and my own toothbrush."

—ELLEN DEGENERES

This was the *last* thing she was expecting.

Fresh out of nursing school, Mom had her whole life ahead of her. She loved spending time with her friends and classmates, especially Margaret. She and Margaret, who was roughly eleven years Mom's senior, had many crazy times together. During one of their escapades, Margaret asked her, "So, Sue, are you dating anyone?"

"Ha-ha, no, I'm not. I just broke up with my boyfriend, Tom, actually. He was a bit of a bore," Mom chuckled.

"Oh, yeah? Sorry to hear that. Ya know, if you're ready to get back on the dating scene, I've got a cute nephew you could meet," Margaret replied with a gleam in her eye—ever the hopeful matchmaker.

Mom tried not to sound too interested, "Oh, really? What's his name?"

"Jeff. And the girls back home say he's pretty cute."

"Is that right? Where's home? Around here?" Mom blushed.

"Well, not exactly. He lives in Montana."

"Montana?" Mom gasped.

Their home states both started with the letter M. That's about all they had in common. She was a city girl from Maryland and him, a country bumpkin from a one-horse town in Eastern Montana. The chances of them meeting were as likely as a trout marrying a sparrow. Only a prayer, some hope, and a little sense of adventure would seal that deal.

That's the exact recipe Mom had in her heart as she embarked on a steel bird headed west. She was brave but sensible, only agreeing to meet her young cowboy suitor in the twin cities of Minnesota. (Besides, it was another "M" state.) This mystery man, who went by the name of Jeff, got into his gray El

Camino and drove east, watching the Rimrocks, and the life he once knew, disappear in the rearview mirror.

She could have stayed in Baltimore and made amends with the yawn of a guy named Tom. She could have had a couple of kids. (I guarantee they wouldn't have been as cool as yours truly.) She could have been happy, too. This Western expedition marked a unique spin on my mother's journey. Again, she could have very easily dismissed Margaret's offer. She had a feeling, though, and this feeling would forever change the course of her life.

Now, as the result of a miraculous twist of fate and a little bit of daring, she was left swooning in the arms of a Montana cattle rancher. What I love most about this story is that Mom starred in her own Hallmark movie (or I should say "Halemark") and she didn't even know it. Her story didn't have a sickening fabricated plot with the perfect small-town backdrop or require C-list actors. Her story was a real love story, one filled with dreams and hopes of starting a family and living happily ever after.

She went on to do all that and more until, sadly, her story was canceled way too soon. In fact, her life's reel had at least twenty-five or thirty years of blank film left, waiting to be pressed with new memories, new dreams, and new adventures. When Mom's sweet body gave out and she left us, my life took an unwanted detour. All of my future plans included her, which made me wonder.…

What do we do with all those dreams, hopes, and plans we had before our loved one died?

Do we just toss them aside?

Do we forget they even existed?

A dear friend of mine, Bob Willis, the author of *A Guide for Grievers*,[29] posted a daily "Mourning Moment" on Facebook that struck a chord with me.

He writes, *"Unfortunately, dreams can be shattered by an illness, an accident, or even a death. Dreams can be destroyed, making it almost impossible to dream again. What can we do now? How do we cope with these intrusive, painful changes?*

"Here is an option," Willis proposed.

"Write down every dream, every wish, and every thought of what 'could have been, what might have been, and what should have been.'

"Keep this journal near, never stop writing, put words to your pain.

"Respect and honor this journal, it contains your broken dreams. Putting words to your pain and writing them in a journal can soften the pain of losing a dream."

In a lot of ways, this book you're holding right now is more or less my "broken dream journal." Commemorating my fondest memories of Mom has been cathartic. Every word,

---

29 Willis, Bob. "From Bob's Heart." Godhealshearts.com, www.god-healshearts.com

every memory, and every story has its place in my healing heart now. In revisiting Mom's fairytale, I became re-inspired to do something I had never intended to do before she died: rewrite my story. I had to do it in a way that honors her but is as unique as the individual hairs on my head.

Not having a clue where to begin, I found inspiration after speaking with "The Social Girl Traveler"[30] herself, Jennifer Morilla. Jennifer was devastated when her brother, Louis, died at the young age of nineteen. Instead of taking time to heal and process his death, she buried her grief. She carried on with her life as if nothing had happened.

She did what was expected of her as a young adult who was about to graduate college. She went on to land an impressive job at a Fortune 500 advertising agency in the heart of Manhattan, with an equally impressive salary. "I had it all. The job, the career, even a super cute guy who I was dating," she said. "I had done everything right and according to plan. But I was miserable."

Her next step was an about-face, and she gave it all up to go on the road.

"I sold every item I had to my name, except a suitcase and a toothbrush," she said. She uprooted her comfy life in New York and headed east to Europe. For the next eight months, she did nothing but travel from country to country, searching for solace amidst the unknown. When she landed in León, she found the healing experience she yearned for.

---

30 Morilla, Jennifer. Socialgirltraveler.com, www.thesocialgirltraveler.com/

In the northwestern tip of Spain, Jen embarked on the walk of a lifetime. El Camino is a five-hundred-mile "jaunt" with the proper name Camino de Santiago.[31] The trail winds its way through the hills of the rural countryside of France and Spain, ultimately leading to a shrine of the Apostle Saint James in the northwestern region of Galicia, Spain. For centuries, people have trekked the Camino de Santiago as a retreat for spiritual growth.

This type of raw, challenging journey resonated with Jen, so she laced up her hiking boots and off she went. "I had no idea what was in store for me over those next two and a half weeks," she said. "I walked, I cried, I wrote, all the while trying to process the death of my brother and best friend." Her emotions went on a walk, too. She wandered from mad to sad, and then to happy. The spiritual impact of her journey hit about halfway through her walk. "That's when I was forced to come to terms with Jesus Christ," she said. "It was a very healing part of the trip for me."

After weeks of walking, she saw the town of Santiago in the distance. The backdrop was one she had hoped for. "All I could see was a beautiful sunset," she said. Just before completing her two-and-a-half-week journey, Jennifer paused for a moment of reflection. Physically and mentally exhausted, she peered over and saw a tranquil pasture with a herd of cattle. Jennifer even remembered birds chirping in the woods nearby.

31 Biggers, Ashley M. "What Should I Know about Hiking Spain's El Camino de Santiago." Outsideonline.com, www.outsideonline.com/1784791/what-should-i-know-about-hiking-spains-el-camino-de-santiago

Her eyes filled with tears, and she began to sob, experiencing all the sadness of Louis' death. The happiness of finishing El Camino flowed over her, and she sobbed even more. She said she felt her brother's presence, and out of nowhere, she took her hands from her face and stopped crying. "His spirit was 1,000 percent palpable," she said, and it signaled to her that he'd never leave her.

That eternal embrace gave Jennifer the strength she needed to pursue her life's work. That moment helped make her journey unique and impactful, and what she chose to do next was for the both of them. She discovered that what she wanted to do with her life was to travel, but with a twist. She wanted to help others while she journeyed. She found a deep-rooted peace in helping other people. "Traveling makes me feel alive," she said. "I wanted to do more than just lend a helping hand. I wanted to be the hand."

But how?

She looked deep into her memory bank and came to one of her most cherished moments with Louis for inspiration. Just weeks before he died, their family took a much-needed vacation to the Bahamas. Jennifer didn't drink before the legal age and never disobeyed her parents. Louis was the polar opposite. "He did what he wanted, and he didn't think twice about the consequences," she said.

"One day, Louis had an idea. He was full of them," she explained. "I remember him saying, 'Let's go get some beer for dinner tonight. It's about thirty minutes outside of town. We can fill up the water jugs while we're at it.'"

Jennifer was leery of her brother's bold request. She was scared to go gallivanting unsupervised in a foreign country, but they did it. And they did it together. They got the beer and filled up the water jugs. What moved Jennifer was one last heart-to-heart with Louis—a conversation she now cherishes. Before returning back to the family vacation house, they cracked open two ice-cold beers, watched the sun set and talked about their plans for the coming year. "Come on, Louis, I shared! Now, it's your turn," Jennifer encouraged her brother. "You're almost a college grad, and you have your entire life ahead of you. Promise me, you'll do something you love."

With a smile on his face, he simply said, "We'll see."

That "We'll see" never came to fruition for Louis. Losing him lit a fire in Jennifer's heart. Grasping onto every detail of her final excursion with her brother, she remembered the water jugs—the secret reason Jennifer used to justify their impulsive trip to town. She might have declined if not for the water mission. In that memory, Jennifer saw her life's vision: to bring water and the gift of sanitation to the world. "All I need is my book bag, laptop, and water filters, and out the door I go," she said.

She could have very easily hidden from her purpose. She could have stayed in New York in her cushy job and life. However, the universe had different plans. She now travels to remote towns all over the world bringing people clean water filters and a bright smile. It makes her soul feel complete. This leap of faith is special because it paved the way for her to land another one of her dream jobs—as a renowned travel blogger.

She braved this unknown world because, she said, she was, "determined to do more of what made her feel good." She did it not only for herself but for her brother Louis, as well.

Sometimes, we have to seek what makes our journey unique to find our true destiny. Mom took a chance on a cattle rancher from Montana. She lived a life that ended up being much more than she had planned. My mother's and Jennifer's stories have given me a lot to think about. I've tested the waters a bit. I've traveled. I've taken risks. However, I'm not sure if I've hit my *good mourning* groove just yet. It is why I decided to write this book: to learn from the greats like Jennifer.

What I am getting is that this journey is different for everybody. Sometimes, it takes a while for our "unique spin" to evolve. For Jennifer, it took years for her to find the answers. It wasn't until she traveled to Europe and walked El Camino that she found what made her life whole. My mom found her cowboy when he rolled up in a slightly different El Camino, and that made her life perfect.

Maybe my unique spin is this book. Maybe it's not. Maybe I'll find my path atop a camel as I ride Sam, Jr. across the United States. Who knows? I haven't given up, and I will keep searching. You should, too.

In the next chapter, we'll learn about Barrett's story of how he uses the practice of rituals to help his hurting family heal from his cousin's death.

First, let's see where we traveled in this chapter...

GOOD MOURNING INSIGHTS

- When your life takes an unwanted detour, strive to find your unique path.
- Put your fears aside and follow your heart.
- In a journal, make an ongoing list of every dream, thought, and plan that could have or should have been. Get them out of your head and onto paper.
- Rewrite your story.

CHAPTER 19

RITUALS—BARRETT'S LIFE ALTAR-ATIONS

———

"This is what rituals are for. We do spiritual ceremonies as human beings in order to create a safe resting place for our most complicated feelings of joy or trauma, so that we don't have to haul those feelings around with us forever, weighing us down."

—ELIZABETH GILBERT

I wanted to marry this coat.

What a great husband it would be, too. Not only would its tri-climate design support me whenever an unexpected storm arose, but its baby-blue exterior would make me weak in the knees. It would even wrap its strong, padded arms around mine and caress my back when no one else would.

The frequency of my "coat husband" fantasy increased steadily leading up to my fifteenth birthday. Though Mom's gift-giving skills were stellar, I couldn't bear the thought of blindly relying on her "intuition" this year. I was reaching the height of my high school career. That meant I had to make sure I was getting *exactly* what I wanted. My popularity depended on it.

Or at least at the time, I thought brand-name materialism moved me up a peg on the social food chain. To me, this coat had exclusive invitations to the cafeteria "cool table" written all over it. Desperately wanting to eat my lunch with the most enviable cliques, I had to bring Mom into the fold of my deep-rooted desires for this coat. And quick.

I started with basic manipulation techniques. Traipsing around her in my baby sister's coat, I claimed "my" coat was too small. She didn't buy it. Well, she did, actually, buy Becky the coat that I was wearing in an attempt to pull the wool over her eyes. "Nice try, Jen," she said as I peeled the slender tan pea coat off my back.

Next, I tried the guilt trip complex, feeding Mom a bill of goods that I was the only girl in school without a "cool coat." She just rolled her eyes and said, "Ya know, if you put this much effort into your studies, you'd have straight A's." Feeling a bit defeated, I knew in the back of my mind she was going to get this coat for me. She just had to.

The day before my birthday arrived, I desperately wanted to see my coat with my own eyes, the coat I knew Mom broke down to buy for her distressed daughter. That's when I did what any bratty teenager would do. I looked for my present.

The moment I walked in the front door from swim practice, even before pouring my oversized bowl of pre-dinner Raisin Bran, and before I took off my sopping-wet sweatpants, I tip-toed ever so quietly to her bedroom. I clenched my feet to avoid making that confounded squish sound from soaked flip-flops hitting the hardwood floor.

I went to the obvious place—her closet. After rummaging from top to bottom, through her shoes, sweaters, and dresses, my beloved coat was nowhere to be found. I was a bit dumb-founded. I threw my wet body on the ground like a seal doing a trick at the Aquarium to sneak a peek under her bed. Nothing but dust bunnies and a stray red sock. Next, it was time to ransack her dresser. No trace of my blue coat anywhere. That's when I started to panic. *Where is my coat?*

It was almost like she could read my mind because she came into the room behind me to say, "Jen, I didn't get a chance to get your coat. I promise I will go get it this weekend," she replied with deep remorse. "Mooommm! Why not? You knew how much I wanted it for my birthday. And, if you don't remember, it's tomorrow!"

She didn't owe me an explanation. She had been busy doing blood pressure screenings for the homeless who lived in the woods behind the high school. All of her good deeds fell on deaf ears as I tore into her like any spoiled-rotten, hor-mone-imbalanced, teenaged girl would.

"Mom, you have ruined my life!" I screamed.

I stormed off to my room and slammed the door. I skipped dinner I was so mad. After crying myself into oblivion, I dozed off on my bed. I awoke when I heard Dad put his springy recliner up to read the paper in the living room. I headed to the kitchen to find it dimly lit with a candle Mom left burning on the counter. I noticed her car keys were missing from the round brown basket, and her car was gone.

"Dad, where is Mom?" I yelled.

"Oh, she ran to the mall. She said she needed to get something for tomorrow."

I knew what that something was, and I was elated. My utter bliss was interrupted when the phone rang. Dad jumped up to grab it and listened for a minute. Then he got very serious and asked the person on the other end, "Are you okay? I'll be right there."

The second he hung up, I asked, "What's wrong?"

"Your mother hit a deer just past the gas station. She's okay. I'm going to go get her."

My heart sank.

"Let me come with you," I said.

"No, you stay here," he replied as he put on his jacket.

I waited with bated breath in the dining room for them to return. Finally, headlights turned into our driveway. Mom crept up the drive in Dad's car and parked in front of the garage.

Then, I saw her car. The hood had a massive deer-sized dent, and the windshield was completely smashed with tufts of brown hair in the cracks. The yellow emergency lights were stuck flashing from the impact. The hand-me-down Oldsmobile had seen its final day.

I flew out the door faster than a cheetah to greet her, "Mom, are you okay?" I asked with a shaky voice.

"Yes, Jen, I'm okay. A little shaken up, but I'm okay."

I timidly walked toward her as tears began to run down my face, "I'm sorry, Mom."

"I know you are, Jen. Go on and go to bed. We have a big day tomorrow," she said.

The next morning, I awoke to the smell of cinnamon buns baking in the oven. She made them for me every birthday. Still feeling guilty about my dramatic performance the day before, I didn't go all the way to the kitchen right away. Instead, I sat at the top of the stairs, peering through the crack in the door to watch Mom put up the multicolored "Happy Birthday" sign she always hung in the bay window. It was a tradition.

After I accidentally banged my head on the banister, she saw me. "Jen, come up here!" she demanded. I walked upstairs to find the living and dining rooms completely transformed into Mom's customary autumn wonderland. It was not only my birthday. It was Thanksgiving, too.

The dining room table with the extended leaf she always brought out on special occasions had a cream-colored lace overlay with eight place settings adorned with her olive green and pumpkin orange filigree bone china—the set she and Dad got for their wedding. The centerpiece was always a cornucopia filled with a bouquet of orange and yellow chrysanthemums with two orange candlesticks in regal gold holders on either side.

"Happy Birthday, Jen!" she exclaimed. "How is my turkey baby? Feel any older?" It was like she had forgotten how I misbehaved the night before. She came over to give me a big hug and kiss on the cheek.

"Thanks, Mom," I replied sheepishly.

She left to go to her room. When she came back, she had a coat-sized bag in her hands. She handed it to me with a toothy grin. I moved the tissue paper very slowly to capture the tiniest little peek, just like Charlie when he tore the corner of the Wonka Bar wrapper, hoping to find the final golden ticket.

I saw something blue. It certainly wasn't old but new. Mom made my birthday wish come true. She got me my coat!

My life was now complete.

I lifted it out of the big "Happy Birthday" bag and hugged it as I swayed it back and forth like a baby. It was finally mine—the coat I would go visit every time we went to the mall and fantasize about round the clock. Mine. I jumped up and hugged her, and then I threw it on as I paraded around the house for the rest of the day. Not wanting any gravy or birthday cake to get on it, I finally put it in my closet for safekeeping.

That beautiful memory flashed through my mind as I happened to stumble upon *the coat* while preparing for a life celebration event on Mom's one-year death anniversary. My family and I hosted it to share her favorite things like chicken parmigiana and pastimes like planting flowers in her garden with her friends. This event helped all of us heal from our loss, too, while honoring the woman we loved so dearly.

As I sat there with the coat, I remembered all those years ago when she had stopped at nothing to get it for me. She even hit a deer getting it. What I now appreciate more than anything is that none of that hindered her desire to observe my birthday and celebrate me and my life. This coat is so much more than a coat to me. It symbolizes a very important lesson Mom taught me: the party must go on. Now, even in death.

Though her life was cut short, it was well lived and should be celebrated just like any holiday or birthday she would feverishly prepare for. Celebrating her life in big ways and small are now a part of my *good mourning* journey. These celebrations are rituals that will allow me to personally honor Mom and the impact she had on my life.

Self-created rituals give us meaning and provide order in our lives, says the author of *Transitions: How Women Embrace Change and Celebrate Life*, Dr. Abigail Brenner, MD.

Brenner writes, *"By creating and performing personally expressive rituals for ourselves, we move freely into our own spiritual lives, taking charge of marking and honoring the transitions, the special moments in our lives that we find significant, in the ways we deem meaningful. Rituals are tools that give us the freedom to take responsibility for the direction and purpose of our lives. Our task is to seize and shape this freedom—consciously, deliberately, and joyfully."* [32]

What I love about Dr. Brenner's viewpoint is that she puts the ownership of our rituals in no one else's lap but our own. We have the personal freedom to exercise our own rituals the way we want. Period. No one else can take that from us. *We* take charge in the moments *we* find significant in the ways *we* deem meaningful. The power lies within each of us to *"seize and shape this freedom"* but do it *"consciously, deliberately, and joyfully."*

That's exactly what Barrett Pitner, founder and philosopher-in-chief of The Sustainable Culture Lab, did. His idea

---

32   Brenner, Abigail. "11 Ways Rituals Help Us Celebrate Our Lives." Psychologytoday.com, www.psychologytoday.com/us/blog/in-flux/201508/11-ways-rituals-help-us-celebrate-our-lives

for a cross-cultural ritual was spawned after the sudden loss of his cousin, Artie, Jr.

Growing up, Barrett was always careful to keep Artie's innocence intact. Especially when Artie inquired about things he didn't quite understand in his big cousin's favorite MTV shows.

"What are they sniffing?" Artie asked.

Without losing a beat, Barrett replied, "Pixy Stix," which is a popular crystallized sugar candy. It seems our answer to death is just as innocent.

"If there's one thing we should know how to be prepared for, the one thing we know is going to happen to all of us, it is death," Barrett said. "But we're not. When my cousin died, my family and I didn't know what to do. We had no structure, no practice, no communal support. We had nothing left of Artie except all of his things."

That's when Barrett had an epiphany that would change the direction of their *good mourning* journey. He and his family would create an altar for Artie.

"For years, my Mexican-American friends have welcomed me into their Day of the Dead, *Día de Los Muertos*, as they built altars to celebrate and remember loved ones who've passed on. Day of the Dead was created by the Aztecs and Mayans thousands of years ago, and many other indigenous cultures from around the world have created similar rituals and traditions," he said.

"They use pictures, candles, clothes, and belongings of their loved ones and often recite prayers, too," said Barrett. "These practices help people cope with the trauma of death while also bringing people together, strengthening their communities and celebrating their culture," he explained.

When he lost Artie, Barrett strongly believes The Day of the Dead provided the structural support he needed to cope with the loss. "This tradition helped me heal, and for the first time, I could see how it could help my family and others outside the Latino and indigenous communities. Mainstream America has nothing like this and we desperately need it."

Barrett is passionate about bringing this tradition into his African American community. He believes "It will create a new and unique opportunity to proactively strengthen and enrich our own rituals, remember black life and celebrate black culture all while building bridges with other American communities."[33]

He's producing a documentary film[34] titled *Altars: A Cross-Cultural Day of the Dead*, in which he embraces the tradition and spirit of this celebration to create a cross-cultural ritual that can benefit and elevate the voices of all American communities.

"Altars can come in all different shapes and sizes. They don't even have to be altars at all. Each family can decide what

---

33 Altars.com, www.altarsfilm.com/videos/altars-a-cross-cultural-day-of-the-dead-pitch-video-w-captions

34 "About Us." Altars.com, www.altarsfilm.com

makes the most sense for them and for their healing," Barrett said.

Just like my "altar" for Mom came in the form of a life celebration event filled with her favorite things, the beauty of using rituals is that they can look and be completely different year after year. "As long as you have some kind of structure in place, the more prepared you will be and, ultimately, the more at peace you'll feel with your loved one's death," he explained.

I encourage you to embrace the idea of using personalized rituals, even altars, to honor your loved one. They can be public or private. They can even be hourly, daily or yearly rituals. They can even be as small as singing "Happy Birthday" to your loved one or wearing the coat they gave you on special occasions. Whatever you decide, your ritual will give you the structure to honor and celebrate your loved one the way you and only you want.

In the next chapter, we'll learn how Nathasha taps into her inner child to live her life free of worry and full of adventure.

First, let's look again at the lessons we've gleaned this chapter...

GOOD MOURNING INSIGHTS
- Rituals provide a structure to honor and celebrate your loved one.
- Creating altars strengthens and enriches our own rituals.

CHAPTER 20

NOSTALGIA— NATHASHA'S FREE SPIRIT

———

"Even though you want to try to, never grow up."

—J.M. BARRIE, *PETER PAN*

Chocolates, in the shapes of tiny police cars and taxis, were our absolute favorite. Something about the shape just made them sweeter.

Or, it could have been the fact it was Mom's way of treating my sisters and me to life's little luxuries to show how much she loved us.

The only place that sold these novelty confections was the candy store in the mall. We had visited there dozens of times, and Mom made each visit special, so much that this became a sacred place for "just us girls" to eat, shop, and play.

She never rushed our lunch together. We would sit and watch the sights on the carousel in the center of the food court as we munched on our nuggets and fries. She drew our attention to the giraffes, horses, and peacocks as they bobbed up and down with excited children on their backs.

Already knowing the answer, she loved to ask, "Girls, do you want to go on the merry-go-round today?"

Our enthusiasm brought her joy. "Yeah! Yay, let's go!" We left our half-eaten kids' meals and ran over to the ticket booth. She trailed behind us with her purse so she could pay our way and help us buckle in on the animal of our choice. She would leave and find her perfect spot to wave at us riding our wild animals on every rotation.

After the carousel, we visited Miss Kitty, the resident clown who carried a massive cloud of colorful mylar balloons. We weren't there to buy one but just to say hello and watch Mom interact with Miss Kitty. That was gift enough for us.

"Wow, Miss Kitty! You've got quite a lovely bunch of balloons today, don't you?" Mom would say.

"Oh, you bet. I've got some really pretty dolphins today. You see them up there by the butterflies?" she'd reply emphatically.

"I see, I see. Very nice. Have a great day! We'll see you next time," Mom would say as we passed on by.

We didn't have to ask where to go next. Mom knew. She took us to our favorite clothing store that had a great slide right inside. My sisters and I flew to the back of the store to hop in line while Mom perused the sales racks. After at least a dozen times down the slide, she corralled us into the fitting room to try on her frugal finds. We had been pacified by our play, so we had no reason to put up a fight about trying on clothes. So, we put them on efficiently and modeled her finds for approval.

The next pitstop would be the pet store—our favorite. We would get our fix of nuzzling the soft bunnies and adorable puppies. We loved to taunt the flippant parrots to see if they'd repeat our silly, childish phrases like, *"I know you are but what am I?"*

She made sure to cross each item off our to-do lists before she tackled her own. That was Mom. She got so much joy from showing us a good time that, to do her own shopping, she would come back alone. Even then, we would beg her to let us come, too. We loved being with her, no matter what.

If I looked up "nostalgia" in my childhood dictionary, this memory would appear first. The entire experience of visiting the mall, eating chocolate cars, and riding the carousel would be memorialized. If I close my eyes, I can feel this memory with all my senses, but mostly, in my heart, with Mom in the center of it all.

When I lost Mom, my inclination was to bury my yearnings for any nostalgic reminders, like my fondest mall excursions. Surprisingly, I couldn't, no matter how much I tried. Instead of fighting it, I visited the mall shortly after she died. It didn't look or even feel the same as it once did. The carousel was gone, too, but none of that mattered. I not only felt at peace being there, but I was happy.

This was a huge stride in the right direction for me on my *good mourning* journey. The mall will forever be a place I can go and relive my childhood and cherish the good times we spent there.

In the article titled, "*Why Looking at a Photo Can Ease Loneliness and Grief,*" Allison Gilbert demystifies the myths surrounding nostalgia, which she defines "*as a sentimental longing for the past.*" She explains that researchers now finally believe that "*being nostalgic may actually make us happier and healthier.*"

She writes, "*According to a recent article in* Trends in Cognitive Sciences, *nostalgia may be a dynamic motivational force. Coauthor Constantine Sedikides, PhD, of the University of Southampton in England, a psychologist who has extensively researched the effects of nostalgia, says fond memories can generate feelings of engagement and self-esteem that leave us more optimistic, inspired, and creative.*"

What a gift nostalgia provides those of us in mourning. By revisiting and reliving memories, we can reverse feelings of inadequacy and tap into the things that matter most to us.

Gilbert continues, "*[Sedikides'] research also suggests another upside that's especially important for the bereaved: Nostalgia may assuage loneliness. Now considered a social emotion like empathy, it can draw us closer to others—the idea being that when we feel an intense bond with loved ones from our past, we're more likely to feel similar bonds with those around us in the present."* [35]

I have a very similar bond with Mom's dear friend, Vickie. She is not only a nurse, but she also has a huge heart like my mom and reminds me of her, too, with her short dark brown hair, painted lips, and beautiful smile. We saw each other in the neighborhood Target one day shortly after Mom's funeral. We hugged each other and chatted about Mom. Then, she looked at me and said, "When your mother dies, you have to grow up."

The moment those words fell on my ears, I knew exactly what she meant. Technically, she *was* right. I can no longer call my mother after a hard day at work or even ask her to bring me chicken noodle soup when I'm feeling under the weather. I knew she was speaking from experience because that's what she had to do when she laid her own sweet mother to rest. As childish as it sounds, the one thing I don't want to do is grow up. I never want to grow up, especially now that my mother is gone. I want to grow "down."

My mother's playful spirit lives in all my childhood memories. She lives on the merry-go-round at the mall. She lives in the sandcastles on the beach at Ocean City. She lives on the swing set on the playground. She lives in every *Lion King* song. She lives in every chocolate car. How could I possibly

---

35   Gilbert, Allison. "Why Looking at a Photo Can Ease Loneliness and Grief." Oprah.com, www.oprah.com/health_wellness/how-nostalgia-re-lieves-loneliness-and-grief

close the door on those beautiful, amazing chapters just because she's gone?

While I will always treasure those sacred memories, she gave me my innocence. I intend to retain it well into my adult years. I don't even want to tell you when I stopped believing in Santa. It rhymes with "dirteen." Even though I had several hints, like his handwriting looking suspiciously like hers or the massive pile of gifts in her bedroom, she cultivated a magical life for my sisters and me. She made sure we were allowed to have the dreams of childhood.

I still cultivate my innocence. This not only makes me feel happy and alive, but it also makes me think of my mom and smile. Every chance I get, I channel my inner child. It's a testament to my upbringing. I'm the one making obnoxious elephant noises in a silent coffee shop or singing silly tunes into the industrial-sized fan at the gym.

Nathasha Alvarez is a girl after my own nostalgic, childish heart.

Born with a rare brittle bone disease, Nathasha defies the odds and blazes her own *good mourning* journey on her trusty wheels, despite the tragic losses of many of her closest friends.

"I grew up with death," she said. "The first death I experienced was my best friend in kindergarten. But the one friend whose death hurt me to my core was Jamie's." She and Nathasha shared the same bone disease. "Jamie was married, she fostered and adopted two kids, she did yoga, she did everything right," Nathasha said. "She played it safe, trying to buy time for herself and for her family, but none of it worked. Jamie died," she said.

Nathasha is determined not to play it safe. The way she honors Jamie and every one of her dear friends she has lost is by doing what she wants when she wants. Her adventures aren't for the faint of heart. When Nathasha turned forty-eight, she signed up for iFly, the indoor skydiving experience. "My family thought I was crazy, but I did it anyway," she said. "I loved every minute of it."

Next, she wanted to travel to Alaska to go whale watching. When she booked her trip, her sisters didn't want her going alone. Nathasha, along with her sister and friend, made their way north together to witness the majestic sea creatures. She waited and waited to see her beloved killer whales but not one surfaced the entire time. Though she was disappointed, she plans to return again one day.

Now, at age fifty, she tests fate every time she blows out her birthday candles. She refuses to allow her disease to hold her back from anything. She's not only a fearless middle school English teacher in Miami, but she's also the mastermind behind *AudacityMagazine.com*,[36] a lifestyle magazine for physically disabled people. It gives a voice to those who are often overlooked. She and her fearless comrades report on taboo topics like politics, relationships, money, travel, and more.

---

36 Alvarez, Nathasha. Audacitymagazine.com, www.audacitymagazine.com/

No dream is too big for Nathasha. The newest glimmer in her eyes is the dream to host her own TV show. "I want to be Oprah on wheels," she said. "I can't wait until the day I tell my guests to look under their seats to find extraordinary gifts." Her light-heartedness keeps her young, and it keeps her alive.

Sometimes our loss can be debilitating. I've often thought about crawling into a hole and hiding. But I've learned our loved ones live on in our childlike wistfulness. As long as we live, they live, so why not do it with as much joy, happiness, and nostalgia as we can? I encourage you to tap into some of your fond memories that bring about nostalgia for you. You'll be surprised at how much better you'll feel as you make your way on your own *good mourning* journey.

In the next chapter, we'll learn how Kinja reinvented himself from the inside out by learning and applying all the valuable lessons his late mother taught him.

Let's take a moment to be nostalgic about what we learned in this chapter...

GOOD MOURNING INSIGHTS

- Don't play your life too safe.
- Nostalgia is not only healing, but it makes you happier and healthier!
- When your loved one dies, you don't have to grow up.
- Fond memories can boost your self-esteem and make you feel optimistic, inspired, and creative.
- Nostalgia lets us create new bonds similar to the ones we had with our lost loved ones.

CHAPTER 21

INVENTION—KINJA'S ALL OVER (RE)CREATION

"Every day, you reinvent yourself. You're always in motion. But you decide every day: forward or backward."

—JAMES ALTUCHER

It was waiting for me. I could feel it.

The moment the bell rang, I sprinted over to my cubby. There it was, underneath my graded spelling test and the annual spaghetti dinner flyer. Nearly fainting at the sight of the glittery pink envelope, I snatched up my very own personalized invitation to my first sleepover. I was afraid it might disappear, or I would wake up and it would have been a dream.

I quickly grazed the handwritten *"Jenny"* in purple crayon on the front envelope before tearing it open. The details didn't matter, really. All I could stare at were just two words: *You're Invited!* The thought that my friend wanted me to celebrate her birthday at her house was thrilling.

"All right, everyone, let's line up at the door. It's time to head to the bus," my teacher announced.

On my long walk to the bus circle, I planned the perfect outfit and pair of pajamas to wear, plus all the goodies and stuffed animals I would bring. Each selection had to have an element of "cool," to ensure I would be a shoo-in for the next sleepover.

The second our bus driver dropped my sisters and me off at the end of the driveway, I sprinted to the front door.

"Mom!" I yelled as I quickly caught my breath.

"I'm in the kitchen!" she screamed back.

"Can I go to my friend's sleepover next Saturday?" I asked with every ounce of hope I could muster.

She gave me her usual mom reply, "We'll see, Jen."

I said, "Pleeeaassseee!" until I had no more air left in my lungs.

"Okay, you can go but I want you to help your father outside a little this weekend."

The second the word "okay" went from her hesitant lips to my eager ears, I bolted to the garage to grab my sleeping bag.

My next stop was the linen closet. I had to find my favorite pillowcase, the red one with the dalmatians all over it, so I could put it on a spare pillow before my sisters got ahold of it. It went into my duffel bag, along with my stuffed animals and PJs.

I was ready.

All I had to do now was hurry up and wait for a whole week. A week in the world of a third grader was practically three hundred years, but I managed. I took time rehearsing funny things to say in front of all my friends and rummaging through Amanda's CDs to pick some to take with me.

The day of the party *finally* arrived.

The only thing left to do was pick up a few harmless rocks for Dad. Thinking it would help pass the time, this bore of a chore did the opposite—it made time officially stop. I ended up in a cycle of picking up a few rocks, then running inside to check the time, then picking up rocks, and so on.

When it was time to go inside for good, I saw my friend's gift, wrapped by Mom and set by the front door. She had placed my overnight bag and pillow next to it. "Jenny, go get ready. You don't want to be late."

I hurled myself down the steps and changed my clothes. "I'm ready!"

"Okay, go hop in the car. I'll be right out," she said.

As we pulled up to the house, we were shocked to see a firetruck with lights blazing out front. I could see in her eyes that Mom was on high alert. Instead of simply dropping me off, she parked and walked me to the front door. There, my friend's mom greeted us with a big smile.

"Oh, hi, Sue and Jenny, how are you?" she said.

"Hi there, I'm a bit concerned about seeing a firetruck in front of your house. Is everything okay?" Mom replied.

"I completely understand, but don't be worried. Our furnace's carbon monoxide alarm went off not too long ago. The firemen just told us we're in the clear," she responded.

Mom reluctantly let me stay. After a quick hug and kiss goodbye, I sprinted inside before she could change her mind.

"Okay, girls, it's time to make pizzas!" my friend's mother said, to which we all shouted, "YAY!" in unison.

We had just sat down to eat our mini personal pan pizzas when there was a knock at the door. My friend hopped up to go see who it was. Then she looked over at me and said, "Jenny, your dad's here."

I was mortified. "My dad?"

I peered around the corner, hoping she had the wrong guy. No luck. It was Dad standing on the porch looking uncomfortable with his hands in his pockets. I was in total disbelief.

Was he there to take me home *before* I had a chance to actually sleep over?

The phone rang and broke the air. My friend's mother jumped up from the dinner table to answer it. "Hi, Sue, yes, I completely understand. It's okay. Yes, Jeff's here. Okay, now, have a good night. Bye-bye."

"Jenny, that was your mom. She's worried about the carbon monoxide scare, so she sent your dad to come pick you up."

"Okay," I replied.

That's all I could say, but I was dying inside. After stalling as long as I could, I crept into the bedroom to collect my belongings. I wanted to stay more than anything. I could only think of all the things I would miss. The stories, the gossip, the fun, the bonding—everything. I was livid with Mom when I got home.

I was too young to understand that her concern was simply keeping me safe. My mother was really protective. There was a lot in her background that had her be this way—one of her brothers had died at a young age. I only appreciated her having Dad pick me up that night when I was older. I could then understand her concern since carbon monoxide is an odorless, poisonous gas.

Given that her action had an effect on her relationship with my friend's mom from that point forward, this really was a selfless act and not an easy decision to make. She made it even though she knew I'd be upset. Frankly, she chose caution over her own friendships. She had no qualms about sacrificing her name in the community if it meant her children were safe. Mom was a wonderful mother. This quandary made her an even better one to me.

Kinja Dixon, the author of *Re-Creationism*,[37] had a mother who made similar decisions in bringing up her son. She made many sacrifices during his young life, each one giving her the chance to create the best life possible for him while she stayed true to being the best mother she could. Some of those sacrifices were decisions she made when he was young that he only appreciated as an adult, like me appreciating my mom's carbon monoxide decision.

Those decisions ultimately propelled Kinja into a life he realized later he did not want to live. "In February 2009, I was a three-hundred-pound functional alcoholic who thought my top sales performance could get me through life," he said. On the surface, he had everything—a great career, international sales awards, and even an early retirement—but he wanted to turn his life around.

After he stripped away his old patterns of thinking, old habits, and old life to start anew, he gradually reinvented the man he always dreamed of becoming. That's when the concept of Re-Creationism was born. He pursues four pillars of self-recreation every single day—health, emotional intelligence, hunger to gain new knowledge, and purpose.

---

37   Dixon, Kinja. Re-creationism, www.re-creationism.com

During Kinja's re-creation journey, his mother became ill with breast cancer. It was then he realized there was a lot he never knew about his family. "During this time, I discovered my mother's backstory and how it led her to live her life the way she did," he said. "I realized she did the best she knew to do for most of her life, which is exactly what I had done, too. I learned a very important lesson: The better off in life you think you are, the more energy needs to be put into your re-creation."

He believes each of us should learn from our environment as a foundation, but it is our responsibility to only use this as a start. "I'm not a special case. I'm just someone who took the signs that my life showed and re-created everything," he said. "Our job is to take our legacies into realms that previous generations couldn't have even imagined. But that rarely happens because our humanity practices cycles of repetition versus cycles of progression—all because we fail to analyze our backgrounds."

When the cancer eventually took his mother's precious life on July 6, 2017, Kinja made an eternal promise to her, "Right now, I promise that every single day, I'm going to continue to be the best example of what you wanted me to be." Since then, he's used his re-creation principles to uphold that promise to her. Because of all the work that he's done, he's finally able to process his mother's death and honor the woman who raised him.

He feels connected to his mother now more than ever as he helps people from all over the world re-create an ever-evolving life through daily creative action. "If I had not had the wake-up call I did to change my habits and analyze my background, I would not be able to use this re-creation model to overhaul my life or the lives of others," he said. Before he begins working with his Re-Creation clients, he simply asks them, "Is your humanity shaping you? Or are you reshaping humanity?" That's because he believes most people are applying a human-being-limited narrative to their unlimited ability.

Those of us in mourning can ask that same exact question. We can let our sadness and grief shape us, or we can reshape our lives and the lives of those around us. Kinja taught me that the highest form of respect to our lost loved ones is to take a good hard look at our lives right now. We first absorb the things we've learned and the sacrifices our loved ones made, and then we do our best to keep what works and change what doesn't in an effort to re-create ourselves one step at a time.

In the next chapter, we'll learn about my sister Amanda's heartwarming story of how becoming a nurse and a mother has helped her stay connected with Mom.

Let's revisit what we learned in this chapter…

GOOD MOURNING INSIGHTS

- Re-Creationism gives you an opportunity to break free of old habits to make room for new, positive ways of being.
- Honor your loved one and the sacrifices they made by becoming the best possible version of yourself.
- Are you applying a human-being-limited narrative to unlimited ability?

CHAPTER 22

NURTURING—AMANDA'S ANGEL CARE

---

*"I attribute my success to this: I
never gave or took an excuse."*

—FLORENCE NIGHTINGALE

Her frog had dysentery.

"Jenny, I mean, Sully, we need more elixir!" Amanda, our family's very own "Dr. Quinn Medicine Woman," yelled to me as she administered the last drop to her incapacitated stuffed frog. The elixir was nothing but Cherry Coke we siphoned from a bottle in the garage refrigerator. It was the only medicine we could get our hands on in the wild frontier of "Colorado Springs" in our backyard of Norrisville, Maryland.

"Did Mom, I mean Colleen, get the rag for the chloroform yet?" Amanda exclaimed.

"I'll go check!" I answered as I poured more cola onto the ground than into the retired whiskey bottle we had found. "Here she is now," I hollered. Amanda wheeled the wagon housing our infirmary of sick patients to the front step to grab supplies from Mom. "Girls, I found some chloroform for you to use," she said, handing Amanda an old pickle jar filled with water.

"I'm not a girl. I'm Sully!" I shouted from the garage.

"Oh, that's right. Sorry, Sully," Mom said to me.

"This will be my hardest operation since I left Boston," Amanda declared. "Little bunny foo-foo's tail has gotta go. It was trampled by a runaway horse."

"Oh, wow, sounds serious, Dr. Quinn," Mom said, concealing her laughter.

"It is very serious," Amanda affirmed. "If you'll excuse us, I have to go work a miracle now." She took the rags and "chloroform" from Mom's grasp and turned the wagon around. I met up with her once I had the elixir bottle replenished, and we journeyed to the field where the cardboard box, I mean operating table, was set up.

"Dr. Quinn and Sully, dinner is in one hour," Mom yelled to us. "And, remember, our show comes on at eight."

"Our show" was *the* show—*Dr. Quinn Medicine Woman*. We looked forward to it every week. On Saturday night, our family gathered to watch Dr. Quinn, Sully, Colleen and the rest of the cast as they braved the rustic life of the wild, wild West. My sisters and I piled on the couch with Mom to get the perfect view while Dad sat reading his newspaper.

He would rather not have subjected himself, a native Westerner, to these shameful, highly dramatized plots of pioneer life. Nonetheless, he enjoyed watching his girls engage with the stories week after week. To pass the time watching the silly scenarios, he often poked fun at how unrealistically pristine Dr. Quinn looked. "You think Annie Oakley curled her hair like that? I don't think so," he would say.

Dad's sarcasm didn't sour my enthusiasm for the show. It certainly didn't affect my laser focus on the town heartthrob, Sully. He was the mountain man version of Fabio with the perfect amount of muscle and charm that'd make any woman swoon. I desperately wanted to be Dr. Quinn, the damsel in distress, whom Sully often saved in the most painfully ridiculous of situations, like untangling her long hair from a nail it had caught on.

My baby sister, Becky, was more pragmatic with her crushes. She liked Dr. Quinn's adopted son, Brian, who was about her age. She appreciated his sense of adventure and keenness for dogs.

While Mom loved the show, she got a kick out of applying her own medical background to critiquing the impracticality behind all of Dr. Quinn's treatments and operations. "There is no way she could give someone an appendectomy by candlelight!" Then in almost the same breath, she made remarks of admiration for Dr. Quinn.

Amanda was different.

She didn't care about the superficialities of the show or its characters. She was always in tune with what made Dr. Quinn a fine doctor—her caring nature, unwavering fortitude, unconditional sacrifices, and compassionate heart.

Because of Amanda's intense observations of Dr. Quinn's loving practices, she was able to adequately portray her in our backyard reenactments. She always knew how and when to use certain medicines and for which ailments. Since I was often in La-La land daydreaming of Sully carrying me back into town with his bare hands, I didn't have a clue how to care for our stuffed patients. Hence, I got stuck refilling the blasted elixir bottle.

Though Dr. Quinn served as a fine role model for Amanda, there was one person she emulated most—our mom. She was not only a skillful nurse, but she had a tender, nurturing heart that made her care stand out among the rest of the hospital staff. She only left when the job was done, never strictly when her shift ended.

Her natural ability to nurture patients was one of the many blessings Mom passed on to Amanda. Though these skills were inside Amanda from birth, she remembers looking up to Mom at a young age and watching her thrive in her occupation. "I looked to my mom as a woman who had a great career with the flexibility she desired to also be a good mother to her children," Amanda said. That realization, along with her fondness of the *"hospital smell"* of Mom's uniform, drove Amanda to follow in her footsteps and become a nurse.

After Amanda graduated from nursing school, she and Mom formed a special nursing bond, allowing them to "talk shop" and share funny stories and care tips with each other. Amanda spent much of her early career at Harford Memorial Hospital where she exhibited exceptional leadership skills. She quickly caught the eye of her superiors and was promoted to head nurse. Mom beamed with pride when Amanda told her the news.

Like Mom, Amanda never sought out these promotions. She earned them just by doing her job to the best of her ability every single day. What set Amanda apart was her giving, caring heart. That is what earned her the "Nurse of the Year Award" at her hospital, an honor for which her family will always be proud of her. Before she received this prestigious award, Amanda's supervisor brought it to our childhood home, so our mom could be part of the celebration though she was very ill.

Near the end of Mom's life, my family and I often felt a bit helpless. Not Amanda. She knew exactly what to do in every situation, just like she did all those years ago tending to her sick frog and tail-amputated bunny as an aspiring Dr. Quinn. Amanda's confidence never once wavered when she was forced on many occasions to administer morphine to our beloved mom when her hospice nurse was unable to visit.

I'll never forget watching Amanda as she tip-toed toward Mom's bed and kneeled down next to her. She gently touched Mom's arm and whispered in her ear, "Hi, Mom. It's Manda. I'm just going to give you a little medicine in your mouth to help you feel better." When she inserted the syringe, she saw

Mom squirm a little. Amanda stayed with her, reassuring her. "Everything's going to be okay, Mom. I love you," all the while holding her hand and rubbing her arm.

Watching her interact with Mom touched my heart. This gentle, warm exchange is just one of the many examples of my eternal gratitude for Amanda. She always knew how to make Mom as comfortable and loved as possible in her final days.

After Mom died, Amanda's nursing focus changed direction. Watching Mom's hospice care nurse, Karin, fueled her desire to become one herself. "I believe being with someone at the end of their life is such a gift. What I love most is I feel like I'm making a difference," Amanda said. As a nurse for one of the most well-respected hospice organizations in Baltimore, Amanda takes much pride in the care she provides patients and their families. "I'm invited into these families and into their stories. You feel like you're being an angel," she said.

Amanda is, without a doubt, an angel. She spends her days listening to the needs of her patients' families as she cares for and manages the symptoms of their terminally ill and dying loved ones. "You have to help the families through this transition. Some are ready, and some are not," she said. While she believes she is helping people at the worst times in their lives, her new angelic career is bittersweet.

"The most challenging part of being a hospice nurse is reliving Mom's death over and over again. When I meet families with three daughters like our family, memories of those final days flood back," Amanda said. "But I don't let my sadness of losing my mom get in the way of doing my job well. Instead,

I use her strength to get me through," she said. In channeling Mom's eternal strength as a nurturer, Amanda's able to have a *good mourning.*

Amanda's nurturing extends without bounds to her children, just like my mother's did. She is a one-of-a-kind mother to Nik and Liddy. She just has a way with them. She is so gentle, caring, and patient. As her sister, it's truly been a beautiful thing to watch Amanda interact and play with them. "When I became a mother, I found a part of me that I didn't even know was missing. Motherhood made me whole," Amanda said. "Taking care of Nik and Liddy and watching them grow up brings me a lot of joy, just like it brought my mom to raise her kids.

"I really feel like motherhood and nursing have filled my happy bucket. Some days it's overflowing with so much love, and that makes me so happy," Amanda said. "Every day isn't always perfect, but taking care of my patients, Nik, Liddy, and my family gives me the strength to know I'm helping someone. It's a struggle at times, but I keep telling myself I'm doing this for a reason."

Amanda's reason for nurturing others helps her feel happy and connected to our mom. Your reason might be totally different. Mine didn't appear until I saw those white, fluffy faces staring back at me saying "Feed me!" Once I began to help my sheep friends, I felt a renewed sense of purpose, giving me a reason to continue feeding and visiting them week after week.

Whether you're the nurturing type or not, I encourage you to choose something, even if it's as small as a house fern, as exotic as a hermit crab, or as silly as a pet rock, to nurture. You could even take the time to visit and cuddle puppies or kittens at a local shelter, swaddle and hold newborn babies or spend time playing games and talking with retirees at a senior citizen center.

Whatever you decide to do, I promise you'll feel the healing benefits of caring for others on your own *good mourning* journey. You might even become someone's angel in the process.

In the next chapter, we'll learn how my dad, Jeff, mends the massive void in his life with family time and more.

First, let's review everything we've learned in this chapter...

GOOD MOURNING INSIGHTS
- Find healing in your caring for others.
- When you nurture someone or something, you're making a difference in their lives.
- Cherry Coke elixir is the most delicious medicine you'll ever take.

CHAPTER 23

GREATNESS—JEFF'S BRAVE NEW WORLD

"The best way out is always through."

—ROBERT FROST

I got it stuck again.

The brand-new John Deere tractor my dad, Jeff, just bought was in the ditch over in the wet ravine—again. As the owners of a Christmas tree farm, the whole family helped out, and I was on tractor duty that day. I almost gave myself a hernia trying to lift, push, and force the two-ton machine out with my bare hands.

I wasn't worried about Dad's reaction. I just hated disappointing him. Absolutely hated it. I gave up when I started seeing stars, and I sprinted over to where Dad was working to tell him the bad news.

"Ummm, Dad, uhhh, I got the tractor stuck down by the trees," I admitted shamefully.

He didn't flinch. Or even react at all.

Dad just turned off his tractor and calmly walked over to survey the damage. Being a rancher's kid, he knew what to do just by looking over the situation. He climbed on the tractor seat and made a few maneuvers at just the right angle to have the tractor easily climb from the hole to flat ground. I watched in amazement as he had it out and up the hill in about thirty seconds.

"Don't drive so close to the edge, Jennifer," he replied sternly with a little wink.

"But, after watching you, I now know how to get it out," I quipped.

I did not inherit Dad's calm at getting out of holes. He could look at any situation and just know what to do. Sometimes I could do that but not usually. And absolutely not this time. I didn't know how to get out of the massive crater of a hole that was Mom's death.

As I lay beside her in her final days, with my head on her pillow, she gently tucked my hair behind my ear, just like when I was her little girl. I looked at her, and she wiped away the tears from my reddened eyes. I don't think she liked to see her fleeting mortality reflected in my frightened face. "I'm worried about your father. Would you keep your eye on him for me?" she requested. "Of course, Mom, but you don't have to worry about that. You're going to be just fine."

She died a month later. As she and I lay there at the end, it had given me comfort to fill her mind and my heart with hope. And when she left us, my heart ached for my dad. Yes, I lost my mother, an irreplaceable person in anyone's life, but what he lost was his rock, his heart, his life. He lost the girl he drove across the country for. I am reluctant to publicly admit this, but I felt sorry for him—a foreign emotion for me, his daughter, to feel for someone as strong as my dad.

I had never before felt the least bit sorry for him. He was my hero, and my hero's heart was broken. The only thing I wanted to do was take away his pain, and I didn't know how. All I could think to do was remember his strength and remind him of it so he could remember it, too. I thought that my believing in his strength would restore him, somehow. I quickly realized he didn't need any reminders. He was just as brave and strong the day Mom died than ever before and continues to be now.

Dad's always been a force to be reckoned with. For as long as I can remember, there was nothing he could not do. I know every child believes their father can do anything. When it comes to my dad, I'm telling you, it's 100 percent true. He considered every problem my sisters and I brought to him with the utmost patience, with the patience of a farmer getting a tractor unstuck from the ditch.

The man is a saint for what we put him through. Like the time he taught me how to drive a stick shift. As we barreled down the hill at fifty-five miles per hour, I accidentally threw the car in second gear. The high-pitched whine of the motor didn't force him to move a muscle. He gently grabbed the shifter and then told me, "Push in the clutch" and he put it in fifth where it belonged. Or the time he bought Amanda a 1966 baby-blue Mustang after she got her license. He willingly took grief from my mother for that purchase for years afterward. He didn't mind. He just wanted to see Amanda happy.

I never stopped believing in my dad, or in his supernatural getting-out-of-a-hole abilities. I still believe he can do anything, even in the post-Mom era—one we all still find so surreal. What I didn't realize about Dad was that he is capable of so much more. I hadn't underestimated him. I just never considered that he could assume Mom's role and do it so well. He has, and he's done a wonderful job. He might not think so and would probably disagree in an unassuming way. What I've found is that he's handled every situation with just as much patience, grace, and love as she would have done.

The truth is, my sisters and I still need our mother. In fact, we'll never stop needing her. We are grown and we have our own lives. Yet, more than ever, we need her nurturing, her guidance, her love, and her support. What's so amazing about my father is that he's given us all these and more. They may not be as direct as she would have provided, but our emotional needs are being met. Luckily for him, we are well acquainted with the birds and the bees, and we've known our "monthly visitor" for quite some time now. He won't have to deal with those womanly duties. But he's always there for whatever life throws our way.

I fell victim to a spam call shortly after Mom died. I bit the bait like the fool I am. If it hadn't been for the amazing workers at the bank and Dad, I probably would be in a hole right now. They cut me loose before it was too late. I was in total dire straits. This is the type of call that I would have typically reserved for my mother. But she was no longer alive to pick up the phone. So, I called my father, crying hysterically. I will always remember what he said next…

"Whatever happens, we're in this together."

I could not have said it better myself. We *are* in this together. We're in the muck of my mother's death together. We're in this tree farm business together. We're in this thing called life together. Watching my sisters and me get closer to my father has been a beautiful experience. Before Mom died, we barely texted. Now, we're on full-blown text chains with him, sharing pictures and emojis like a bunch of pre-teen millennials.

We share a lot more. I love to coerce my father into going to country music concerts with me—ones he likes and ones he doesn't! I dragged him all the way to a tiny town in northern Minnesota last February to see Gretchen Wilson. While getting there was the biggest pain in the cold arse, it was worth every penny, every mile, and every shiver.

When we arrived, we had one of the most heartfelt conversations about my mother we've ever had. A little wine helped us both open up. The remarkable thing is, once Dad got going, he didn't stop talking, reminiscing, and honoring the woman he loved. "She was a hot chick who was out of my league," he said. "Right after we met, she came to Montana and wore this real flowery blouse. After seeing how gray Montana was, she was always embarrassed about having worn the wrong blouse. I didn't care what she wore. I was just happy to see her."

Boy, did she make him happy. "I never did much Montana touring before I met your mother. Then, I got to show it off to her. We went to Yellowstone and toured Glacier Park. She loved seeing the little mountain goats sliding down the snowbanks. I just loved seeing her smile. We went to visit Grandma Hale, too. She made us her famous goulash, which Sue loved, that was until she found out the 'beef' was actually elk," he laughed. "She put her fork down so fast. She always knew what she wanted and it wasn't elk."

The one thing Mom wanted more than anything was to become a mother. Afflicted with endometriosis, she needed surgery to make her dream happen. Dad remembered spending the day at the hospital with her before surgery. "As I was walking out of the hospital, I looked back and there was Sue looking out the window of the waiting room waving at me. It was this forlorn 'why are you leaving me?' kind of wave. I can still see her in that window tugging at my heart, and that happened forty years ago.

"When I saw her holding you babies for the first time," he paused, "that was a big deal," Dad reminisced. "Ocean City was always so fun. Christmas, too. Your mother was the quintessential Santa Claus," he chuckled. "Staying up into the wee hours of the morning wrapping presents and displaying them just so for you girls under the tree.

"She left me lots of good stuff, so I'm blessed. Three lovely daughters. Great memories. The joys and heartaches of being with her for thirty-seven years," Dad said. "We have to carry on. We have to fill in the void she left. She didn't want to leave, but she would have wanted us to carry on the best we can."

My mom left some pretty big generous footsteps for me and my sisters to follow in. Once when she got money from her late Uncle Marvin, she dragged my dad down to the electronics store and bought the family a huge flat-screen TV that we still have. Back then, they were very expensive. It was $3,500, and it was something she wanted to do.

To pay homage to her, we love to love on our dad. We love to buy him his favorite maple cream cookies, take him out to dinner, and spend time with him every chance we get. It's not because we feel obligated. It's because we want to show him how much he means to us. We want him to know how much we appreciate what he's done to be our father, and now, our mother, too.

Dad has always been an independent man. Being a clingy husband just wasn't a part of his blood. He and my mother had a special marriage where they both had their own individuality but loved each other deeply. The one thing my dad has had to reimagine is his life without her. He's had to find his own stride again. He's had to discover what makes him tick, what brings him joy, and what gives him the strength to keep living.

While Dad always traveled for work, Mom was never fond of flying or traveling, for that matter. To honor her wishes, he didn't plan many trips to exotic places. He instead made arrangements for local weekend excursions to Williamsburg, their honeymoon destination. However, since she's died, he's done a fair amount of exploring new regions like Key West, Mississippi, and parts of Germany, too. Though he curses the plane rides, he enjoys his adventures with his buddy, Rob.

He's even dusted off old pastimes like square dancing, which he had enjoyed as a young man before he met my mother. He used to square dance at his local Montana grade school, but she threw a monkey wrench in those outings. Three kids, a thirty-seven-year-long marriage, a house, a tree farm, and a successful career later, I don't think he minded.

I was so pleased to find out he has picked it back up again after a four-decade hiatus. The one thing my dad does well is once he puts his mind to something, he sticks with it. He makes sure he doesn't miss his lessons. He even partakes in the themed dances like the Halloween Hoe-down where he dressed up as a cowboy. Dad's sense of humor accessorized the outfit, which was equipped with an "assault" banana in his holster and Dum Dum lollipops in his bullet clip.

Whether we believe it or not, we're all destined for greatness on our *good mourning* journey. The greatness I'm talking about doesn't require you to be a warrior who walks around with a sword and shield all day. Greatness simply means having the courage to keep moving forward in your life despite your loss.

Dad's greatness lies in his choice to spend quality time with his family, continue being the best father and grandfather he can, travel to new, fun places, and even revisit fun, nostalgic hobbies like square dancing. He does it all with a smile on his face, but most of all, with courage in his heart.

The death of our loved ones can knock us down, but it's up to us to decide how we handle it. We can get all tied up in our sad, debilitating grief and let it ruin our lives. Or we can mourn our loss with every ounce of courage, strength, happiness, and joy we can, bettering our own lives and those we love in the process.

The choice is yours. Choose greatness.

GOOD MOURNING INSIGHTS

- When we're faced with doing the best we can, we aim even higher.
- Find your own stride again.
- Discover what makes you tick, what brings you joy, what gives you the strength to keep living.
- Remember, you can get out of the hole.

READY, SET, *HAVE* A GOOD *MOURNING*

———

"This is not a dress rehearsal; this is your life."

—BILL MURRAY

If there was one line Mom said to me again and again...

It was this Bill Murray quote.

I can still hear her saying, "Jen, this is not a dress rehearsal. This is your life." No matter when or where, if I came to Mom with a problem, this dress rehearsal line would always be part of her spiel. She told me so many times, I often dismissed it, thinking, *Yeah, yeah, Mom. I know. My life is not a dress rehearsal.*

I didn't believe this quote, that my life was not a dress rehearsal, until I buried my mom's sweet, precious body on April 30, 2018. Now that she's gone, I relish her wise advice.

I've given it a lot of thought, actually. What her adage means to me is: If you want to do something, DO IT. Don't wait until the best optimal moment because it will never come.

Mom didn't think she would die at sixty-four. But she did. And for those sixty-four years, she walked her talk. She lived her best life and cherished the people around her. Now, the best thing I can do for her is to live my life to the fullest.

The truth is we don't get a second chance. My mother didn't get a second chance when she was diagnosed with cancer. In fact, her story ended too soon. She was gone before her time. When her life ended, I faced the greatest loss in my life so far. She meant the world to me.

I sought ways to manage my grief. As I mentioned earlier, I tried all the traditional paths, and they weren't what I needed. They did not help me fill the massive void she left, nor did it help me create my life without her. They bogged me down by having me harp on my grief and remain in a dark, depressing place for too long. I didn't want to dwell in my grief or sit in grief traps waiting for my life to begin again.

That's when I decided I would *Have a Good Mourning.* I saw my mourning as a journey, and that journey would lead me back to myself. When I created this way of finding joy inside my grief and authored this book to share it with you, I was first thinking of myself. Now I am thinking of you. Your journey may be something like mine or nothing like mine. Nonetheless, I hope you found ways to nurture yourself and bring yourself joy in the face of your loss.

I've given you seventeen different techniques to create "What's next?" on your *good mourning* journey. I urge you to take them on and create practices to inspire yourself and those around you. If you need a little help getting started, I am happy to help you brainstorm. Your next step could be a variety of fun, exhilarating things, like...

- Taking a cooking class in Tuscany because your father loved Italian food...
- Volunteering at a ferret refuge because your aunt bought you one for your birthday as a kid...
- Buying an ice cream cone for an elderly person and talking with them for hours about "the good ole days" because you miss your grandma...
- Taking a hot-air balloon ride across California because your uncle loved to drive the seacoast...
- Visiting and feeding camels on a regular basis to feel a sense of purpose...
- Cashing your check and taking your kids to Chuck E. Cheese because your mother used to do that for you...
- Taking a bike ride with your buddies and yelling "squirrel!" for the duration of the hundred-mile trek...
- Acting like a goofball when it's not called for...
- Nurturing a pet lizard you adopted for the first time...
- Dusting off an old hobby you used to enjoy, like square dancing...

The first step on your *good mourning* journey could be any number of things. Whatever you think of doing, do it. Don't wait. I promise, what you choose will lead to the healing you desperately desire.

When grief strikes, open this book again. Pick one of the letters of the *Have a Good Mourning* acrostic and turn to that chapter. Read the whole story, or just refresh the tips and insights at the end. Whatever you choose, take action and get on with your life. This is the real thing.

Through these ideas, my hope is you carry on with joy, courage, and inspiration, and bring the same to people in your life.

The biggest lesson my mom taught me was that life is not a dress rehearsal. To me, that means I should not worry and focus on the mistakes of my past. It means to enjoy every part of my day and this moment because that's all I have.

If we who are left behind have the choice to mourn joyfully, that will help us get that second chance at living our best life. We will get there faster if we don't wallow in our grief for too long.

Dear reader, my advice to you is to cherish the people in your life, don't wait to do what brings you joy, and pass that joy along to others.

Most of all, have a *good mourning.*

APPENDIX

"50 Kindness Ideas for Random Acts of Kindness Day." Randomactsofkindness.org, www.randomactsofkindness.org/the-kindness-blog/2943-50-kindness-ideas-for-random-acts-of-kindness-day

"About Us." Altars.com, www.altarsfilm.com

"About Us." Goodnewsnetwork.com, www.goodnewsnetwork.org

Altars.com, www.altarsfilm.com/videos/altars-a-cross-cultural-day-of-the-dead-pitch-video-w-captions

Alvarez, Nathasha. Audacitymagazine.com, www.audacitymagazine.com/

Baltussen, Han. "Coping with Bereavement and Grief: Lessons from History." Theconversation.com, www.theconversation.com/coping-with-bereavement-and-grief-lessons-from-history-9088

Biggers, Ashley M. "What Should I Know about Hiking Spain's El Camino de Santiago." Outsideonline.com, www.outsideonline.com/1784791/what-should-i-know-about-hiking-spains-el-camino-de-santiago

Brenner, Abigail. "11 Ways Rituals Help Us Celebrate Our Lives." Psychologytoday.com, www.psychologytoday.com/us/blog/in-flux/201508/11-ways-rituals-help-us-celebrate-our-lives

"Brief History of Grief and the Five Stages." Grief.com, www.grief.com/the-history/

Brock, Farnoosh. "The Importance of Practice: Use it or Lost it. Prolificliving.com, www.prolificliving.com/the-importance-of-practice-use-it-or-lose-it/

Corbley, McKinley. "American Brothers Successfully Save Irish Girl Who Was Swept out to Sea in Serendipitous Twist of Fate." Goodnewsnetwork.org, www.goodnewsnetwork.org/brothers-save-irish-girl-at-sea-in-serendipitous-twist-of-fate/

Corbley, McKinley. "VHS Tape of Baby Taking First Steps Is Finally Returned to Family After Man Found It inside a Used TV." Goodnewsnetwork.org, www.goodnewsnetwork.org/vhs-tape-of-baby-taking-first-steps-returned-to-family/

Dacre Balsdon, John P.V., and Ferguson, John. Marcus Tullius Cicero." Britannica.com, https://www.britannica.com/biography/Cicero

Davenport, Barrie. "10 Life-Altering Mind Shifts to Rock Your World." Pickthebrain.com, www.pickthebrain.com/blog/10-life-altering-mind-shifts-to-rock-your-world/

Dixon, Kinja. Re-creationism, www.re-creationism.com

Erickson, Angela. "14 Things You Probably Didn't Know About C.S. Lewis," Bookbub.com, www.bookbub.com/blog/facts-about-cs-lewis

Feldman, David B. "Why the Five Stages of Grief Are Wrong." Psychologytoday.com, www.psychologytoday.com/us/blog/supersurvivors/201707/why-the-five-stages-grief-are-wrong

Firestone, Lisa. "Why Generosity Is Good for You!" Psychalive.org, www.psychalive.org/why-generosity-is-good-for-you/

Gazibara, Steve. "The Chances of You Being Born You Are 1 in 400 Trillion, Act Like the Miracle You Are." Whiskeyriff.com, www.whiskeyriff.com/2016/09/29/the-chances-of-you-being-born-you-are-1-in-400-trillion-act-like-the-miracle-you-are/

Gilbert, Allison. "Why Looking at a Photo Can Ease Loneliness and Grief." Oprah.com, www.oprah.com/health_wellness/how-nostalgia-relieves-loneliness-and-grief

Gill, N.S. "The Six Types of Togas Worn in Ancient Rome." Thoughtco.com, www.thoughtco.com/six-types-of-toga-in-ancient-rome-117805

"Good Morning, Good Life: An Interview with Amy Landino." Dailystoic.com, https://dailystoic.com/amy-landino-interview/

Grimm, David. "How Dogs Stole Our Hearts." Sciencemag.com, www.sciencemag.org/news/2015/04/how-dogs-stole-our-hearts

Hoyt, Alia. "How Grief Works." Science.howstuffworks.com, www.science.howstuffworks.com/life/grief1.htm

Kirk, Julie. "Death Rituals." Dying.lovetoknow.com, www.dying.lovetoknow.com/Death_Rituals

Kloppers, Mandy. "Too Much Pretending." Mentalhelp.net, www.mentalhelp.net/blogs/too-much-pretending/

Lewis, C.S. "A Grief Observed Quotes." Goodreads.com, www.goodreads.com/work/quotes/894384-a-grief-observed

Medindia Content Team. "World Death Clock." Medindia.net, www.medindia.net/patients/calculators/world-death-clock.asp

Morilla, Jennifer. Socialgirltraveler.com, www.thesocialgirltraveler.com/

"Rather Than Slip into Depression, Man Quits Job, Sells Possessions, and Travels the World with a Ferret." Goodnewsnetwork.org, www.goodnewsnetwork.org/airman-quits-job-and-travels-world-with-ferret/

Scientificamerican.com, www.scientificamerican.com/article/five-fallacies-of-grief/

Shermer, Michael. "Five Fallacies of Grief: Debunking Psychological Stages."

Steinke-Baumgard, Michelle. "Stifled Grief: How the West Has It Wrong." Huffpost.com, www.huffpost.com/entry/stifled-grief-how-the-wes_b_10243026

Tesalona, Michael. "Leave Your Light On; Compassion in a Time of Grief." Ted.com, https://www.ted.com/talks/michael_tesalona_leave_your_light_on_compassion_in_a_time_of_grief

"Tullia" (daughter of Cicero). Wikipedia.org, www.en.wikipedia.org/wiki/Tullia_(daughter_of_Cicero)

Verma, Prakhar. "Destroy Negativity from Your Mind with This Simple Exercise." Medium.com, www. medium.com/the-mission/a-practical-hack-to-combat-negative-thoughts-in-2-minutes-or-less-cc3d1bddb3af

Willis, Bob. "From Bob's Heart." Godhealshearts.com, www.godhealshearts.com

Made in the USA
Columbia, SC
26 April 2020